Valley of the Steeples

How Jesus saved us from Christianity

Brian J. Hennessy

"It's for freedom Christ set us free!"

Brian Hennessy

Ketch Publishing
Bloomington, Indiana

Copyright © 2008

Brian J. Hennessy

ISBN: 978-0-9801420-7-5

Printed and Bound in the
United States of America
All rights reserved.

Except where otherwise indicated,
Scripture quotations used in the book are
taken from the New International Version.

Most names and places mentioned
in this book are true, but a few names
have been changed.

Cover Design by Allen Ketchersid

Ketch Publishing
4675 N. Benton Dr.
Bloomington, Indiana

www.KetchPublishing.com

*To Mo, my amazing wife,
who walked with me
through discouragement and doubt,
disobedience and drought,
and believed when no one else could or would.
Without her extraordinary faith,
courage, love and perseverance,
there would be no story to tell.*

Issues
- A 2nd baptism of the Spirit
- using bible verses as guidance on future direction and leadings.
- (pg 132) - use of a "fleece".
- (pg 97) - being told he was a "prophet".
- - focus on speaking in tongues ("prayer language")

Acknowledgements

I am so thankful to my Heavenly Father who rescued me from my religious mindset, led me to His Son Jesus, and gave me His Holy Spirit.

I also want to acknowledge all those courageous men and women who confronted the falseness of the church system in every century, often at the cost of their own lives.

And I will be eternally grateful to all those friends, relatives and strangers who blessed us and encouraged us along the way when we needed it most.

"Truly, I say to you, there is no one who has left home or brothers or sisters or mothers or fathers or children or farms, for My sake and for the gospel's sake, but that he shall receive a hundred times as much now in the present age, houses and brothers and sisters and mothers and children and farms, along with persecutions; and in the world to come, eternal life."

(Mark 10:29,30; Luke 18:29,30; Matt. 19:29 NAS)

Table of Contents

The Vision 2

Chapter 1 – Heaven Knocks 8

Chapter 2 – The First Encounter 18

Chapter 3 – Adjusting to New Realities 28

Chapter 4 – Tongues of Fire 36

Chapter 5 – The Bridge Church 50

Chapter 6 – Madison Avenue and God 62

Chapter 7 – California Dreamin' 76

Chapter 8 – The Calling 90

Chapter 9 – Down On the Farm 104

Chapter 10 – The Sabbath Rest 122

Chapter 11 – Joy Comes In the Morning 134

Chapter 12 – The Last Church 144

Chapter 13 – Reflections 158

Chapter 14 – A New Beginning 170

A Word to the Wise 182

The Vision

The vision came the way visions do.

Unsolicited.

Without warning.

In the middle of one of life's activities.

One moment my wife was seeing the world as it was. In the next she was viewing a totally different scene. Like someone just switched the channel on her eyeballs.

It was a spring morning in 1976. I had already left for work and Mo (short for Maureen) was busy making the bed at our home in Stamford, Connecticut. That's when God hit the channel changer.

Suddenly the bedroom vanished before Mo's eyes and in its place was a beautiful green valley. In the cleft of the valley she saw Christian churches of all shapes and sizes clustered together, representing every denomination. The one thing they all had in common though, was a steeple. There were no other structures visible.

Then Mo saw Jesus. He was sitting on a grassy hillside with his hands clasped around both knees gazing down at the churches. As she looked at Jesus, He slowly turned to her and His face came closer. She saw He was crying. With great sadness in His voice He said to her, *"I'm not in there."*

As she heard those words she felt the depth of his sorrow wash over her and she began to weep as well. Then the scene faded and the bedroom came back into focus. Having fallen to her knees, she stayed there for awhile with tears running down her face in awe of what she had just experienced. Wondering what it all meant.

When I got home that night, Mo told me of her vision. I had no trouble accepting her experience as genuine, but I was as perplexed as she was concerning its message. We figured it had to be important, or why would Jesus give us this vision? But what did He mean He wasn't in those churches? They were Christian weren't they? And if He is not in them, where is He?

What made the vision even more puzzling was that we had just switched to a wonderful church in search of more spiritual life. We had left a Roman Catholic church, the denomination in which we'd both been raised, and had started attending a charismatic Episcopal church that we considered truly alive with the Spirit of God. In fact, we were so happy with St. Paul's we'd go several times a week just to hear the anointed teaching, join in the joyous singing and experience the loving fellowship we found there. Did the vision mean that Jesus wasn't in St. Paul's, either? How could that be?

This vision marked the latest in a series of extraordinary supernatural events that had overtaken us in the last three years. As a result, our life had undergone a dramatic spiritual realignment as we awakened to the difference between what I'd call dead, rote religion and having a real, living relationship with the Creator of the universe through faith in Jesus Christ. But like any new experience we were still trying to sort it all out. And this vision was now one more piece that needed to be fit into the puzzle.

Although we didn't know it then, our awakening to the things of God had only just begun. We were about to be completely uprooted from our comfortable, middle-class lifestyle and sent on a six-year, cross-country, faith-filled adventure that would change us and our four children forever.

This adventure, which would witness God's miraculous provision and guidance, would reveal to us the startling truth that Jesus did not come to start a new religion called Christianity. He did not come to start any religion at all. He came to set us free from *all* religion with its rituals, traditions, and legal requirements, including the one and only religion God ever gave His people, the Mosaic Law. All He asked us to do now is allow Him to live His life through us and walk in obedience.

In time we would understand and accept the message of the vision at face value. As Jesus plainly said, He isn't in our churches. Most of His people are found in there. His words, as recorded in the Bible, are usually quoted in there. And His Name is repeatedly mentioned. But He is missing. Men and their traditions are being served instead!

Later we found this clearly confirmed in the Word of God. For the Bible states, *"However, the Most High does not dwell in houses* (religious buildings) *made with human hands; as the prophet says: 'Heaven is My throne, and earth is the footstool of My feet, what kind of house will you build for Me, says the Lord?'"* (Acts 7:48,49, NAS). Although He had allowed His people to build Him a stone temple under the first covenant, it was never meant to be more than a picture, an interim step pointing to a future, more intimate place of worship when He would literally be able to dwell in the midst of us.

After Jesus introduced the New Covenant, God allowed the old temple to be removed in 70 AD to make way for this new and greater revelation. As the Bible teaches, He now literally dwells inside His people. We are now the temple of

God. *"Don't you know that you yourselves are God's temple and that God's Spirit lives in you?"* (1 Cor. 3:16). So our bodies are the only place on earth now where God is officially present. In other words, Jesus has left the building.

This book, then, is the story of how God helped us to escape completely from the religion of Christianity that had imprisoned countless millions of families like ours since the fourth century. He set us free in both practice and conscience so that we were never again tempted or intimidated into joining any part of that church system again—whether Catholic or Protestant.

Later the Lord showed us who we really were. Not members of a Gentile religion called Christianity, but physically and spiritually part of the chosen family of Abraham, who taken together, whether Jew or Gentile, are called Israel." *If you belong to Christ, then you are Abraham's seed, and heirs according to the promise"* (Gal. 3:29).

I realize that not everyone will consider the message of this book good news. Many sincerely believe institutional Christianity with its church buildings, holy days, professional clergy, planned worship services and hierarchical organization is what Jesus ordained to help us live out our New Covenant lives. And they cannot imagine any other way to serve Him. Others have invested their whole careers and fortunes in this traditional form of religion and are equally as committed to maintaining the status quo. That is the way it has been down through the centuries. And I suspect that is the way it will remain until the Lord returns to destroy this false hope once and for all.

But I also know there are tens of thousands of other believers out there, clergy and laity alike, who are struggling to reconcile their lives in Christ with their so-called life in the institutional church system. And there are tens of thousands more, having been drawn to the claims of Jesus, who are reluctant to accept him because it means having to join a self-righteous religion they want no part of.

To all of you we offer our story as a beacon of hope and encouragement.

The message of this book, which covers the period between 1973 and 1982, can be summed up with this one Scripture: *"It was for freedom that Christ set us free; therefore keep standing firm and do not be subject again to a yoke of slavery"* (Gal. 5:1, NAS).

Chapter 1

Heaven Knocks

It was Friday, it was lunchtime, and I was hungry. Shutting off my typewriter, I grabbed my jacket hanging on the back of my office door and headed for the elevator. If I hurried, I could still find a seat at Kilroy's Bar and Grill, my favorite lunchtime restaurant.

Located just a block from the advertising agency where I worked, Kilroy's was a New York version of the TV show, Cheers. The owner was an affable, barrel-chested bartender named Irv who always remembered your name and welcomed you with a smile and a handshake. The sandwiches, which hardly ever changed on the menu, were generous and tasty. The conversation was plentiful. And the prices weren't greedy. Put it all together and it meant the place was always packed. So if you didn't get there early to claim a seat, you ate your lunch standing up.

The bar had long been a hangout for a number of art directors and copywriters, who worked in the creative department of our company. For years I had deliberately avoided the place because I'd seen how a few drinks at lunchtime affected the work of those who imbibed regularly. It wasn't much fun working with someone—or worse, for someone—who came back with a lunchtime buzz. But the lure of companionship and a taste for beer that had started in high school had overcome my earlier, wiser decision. And eventually I had just followed the crowd to Kilroy's.

Walking through the door into a room full of noisy chatter, I spotted an open stool at the bar and quickly squeezed in. I said "Hi" to Irv, who drew a beer from the tap and took my order for a hot pastrami on rye, my favorite sandwich. Sitting to my right this day were two men I knew casually from the office. One was a copywriter, like myself; the other a free-lance photographer. Before long we were all three chatting away about the pennant chances of the Mets and other hot topics of the day. I didn't have much work waiting for me back at the office, so after finishing my sandwich, I gave myself permission to have one more beer and continued talking to my two lunchtime companions.

Soon the topic of our conversation transitioned somehow to a discussion about the existence of God. Both men quickly revealed themselves to be atheists, although the photographer preferred to call himself an agnostic. Since I had always believed there was a God, it quickly became two against one.

Both argued that when I got older I would see God was just like Santa Claus, a childhood carry over. Better to realize that now, they suggested, and get on with my life free of all such silly superstitions. Insulated by sixteen years of Catholic schooling, I was a bit shocked by their irreverence. In response, I resorted to the arguments of Thomas Aquinas, whose tome, the <u>Summa Theologica</u>, I had lugged around college for two semesters. It felt good to finally put St. Thomas to work as I hit them with his logic of the uncaused cause that in my opinion gave irrefutable proof of God's existence.

It went back and forth like that for awhile until a very strange thing occurred. I suddenly found myself totally removed from the conversation. That is, my mouth continued to talk, but I became like a third party listening closely to the words I was speaking. As I listened I was struck by how thin my words sounded. Not that they weren't true, but I realized for the first time that everything I knew about God I'd learned from someone else—my parents, teachers, nuns, priests, Thomas Aquinas, etc. I actually had no personal, first-hand knowledge of God at all. All I knew about Him was hearsay.

In that same moment, I also became shamefully aware of how shallow my Christianity really was. Here I was defending God like I was His lawyer, but the truth was my life was a very poor example of someone who called himself a follower. I saw my whole religion like a raincoat I put on a Sunday, and took off on Monday. The rest of the week, every thought and activity had a completely different focus. And if I was really honest, even on Sunday my piety probably lasted about as long as it took me to get through the church service. I was undone. I could see what a hypocrite I was.

I left that lunch shaken to the core. I knew something profound had just happened to me, but now what do I do? As I stood at the curb waiting for the light to change, I resolved before taking another step I would get to the bottom of the matter. Is there a God? If so, how do I find Him? Or Her? What about my religion of Roman Catholicism? Was that for real? I had to have the answers. I determined to climb every mountain and ford every stream, if necessary, to learn the truth.

I was fairly certain God did exist. Over the course of my life I'd sensed His divine hand intervening on my behalf several times. I remembered following two friends home from a party one rainy night after too many beers. As I crested a hill at a high rate of speed in my Pontiac LeMans convertible, I was stunned to see my friend's cars parked at a red light fifty yards in front of me. Realizing I couldn't stop in time, I just slammed on my brakes and ducked. My car went into a spinning, out-of-control power slide on the wet pavement, but instead of crashing, I came to a slow, sliding stop, ending with a gentle bump against the curb. When I opened my eyes and looked around, I was directly across from my friend's cars—but facing the other direction. They were staring at me with mouths open. I felt like angels had just guided me to safety.

Then there was also the way I got into advertising as a career. Graduating from college, I still didn't have a clue about what career path to take. So I postponed the decision and took a job as a busboy at an Inn on Cape Cod for the summer. I eventually wound up as the day bartender in the Inn's cocktail lounge. One afternoon, when I was alone in the bar, a man walked in, plopped himself on a stool and ordered a drink. After fixing it for him, I went back to working on a humorous skit I was writing. I must have been chuckling to myself, because he asked me what I was writing that was so funny. So I told him. Out of the blue he asked, "Have you ever thought of becoming an advertising copywriter?"

"No," I replied, "what's that?" It sounded like some kind of legal position to me. Although my father was in advertising, he was in the financial end, and I never recalled him mentioning the term. When he told me it involved coming up with ideas for ads and TV commercials and then writing the copy, I knew instantly that's what I wanted to do. So when my summer job ended I went straight to New York and soon landed a starting position in a brand new agency. That itself was a miracle, since there are very few openings in that profession.

No, I felt someone was definitely up there and watching over me—but now I needed more tangible proof.

When I got home that night I told Mo about my experience at lunch. I said I needed to find some time to get away and think about God to get some answers. She reminded me that our parish was having a one-day retreat the following morning. She'd mentioned it to me about a week ago, but at the time I wasn't the least bit interested. Now it sounded just like what I was looking for. I decided to attend.

Arriving at the church the next morning, I spotted several men in the parking lot and followed them into the rectory where the retreat was being held. Inside, about 15 men were standing around chatting. I assumed all attended my church, but I didn't recognize any of the faces. This wasn't surprising, since we had just moved into this parish recently and didn't know many people yet. Taking my seat in one of the metal folding chairs that had been set up for the occasion, I wondered if any of these men were on a search like I was. Or were they just naturally religious and attended these kinds of events all the time? Since Mass was the only thing I attended regularly, I felt a little out of my element in this gathering. I decided to just keep to myself, hoping I would catch on to this religious stuff once things got started.

Finally the pastor came in and introduced the speaker, Bob Vogel, a former football player for the Baltimore Colts. I'd never heard of him before, but I wasn't a big football fan, either. But one thing was clear. If I had any thoughts this meeting was for religious namby-pambies, his tall, muscular frame immediately put all such thoughts to rest.

I'll never forget Bob's opening remark. It couldn't have hit me any harder if he'd tackled me. He said, "Jesus Christ is the most important person in my life." And he said it like he knew Him! Like He was a personal friend! He went on to describe how he and his wife would spend their weekends having Bible studies in their home with friends. He said they actually considered this more fun than having parties! My head was spinning! In all my life I'd never heard even a priest talk like this, much less a "layman." At one point he even challenged those of us who were commuters to get a big white Bible and read it on the train going to work each day. It sounded like a new definition for courage to me.

Although I couldn't relate in the slightest to anything Bob Vogel was talking about, I did feel a strange sense of encouragement welling up within me. It was like a small voice was saying, *"See? There are people who believe in Me...who even know Me. Keep searching... you're on the right track."*

The first step in my quest to discover God was to begin changing some of my bad habits. I felt that some of these things I'd been doing were inconsistent for someone who wanted to get closer to God. So I cut way back on my beer drinking, quit smoking, cleaned up my language—which was often quite colorful, and eliminated my occasional purchase of a copy of Playboy.

On the positive side, I began stopping in at a small Catholic chapel on the way to work. I'd slip into a pew, pray for awhile and then before leaving, purchase a small paperback book from a rack at the back of the church. Over the next few months I devoured almost every book they offered. Books about the lives of different saints, the writings of St. Augustine, Teilhard de Chardin, Bishop Sheen, Thomas a Kempis, Blaise Pascal, the miraculous stories of Fatima and Lourdes, the musings of mystics like St. John of the Cross, Thomas Merton and Theresa of Avila, the teachings of several theologians, a number of devotionals, and a papal encyclical or two, to list just a few. I'm sure the church bookstore thought a revival was breaking out. But it was just me.

One book that really grabbed my attention was by a French doctor who had done some unorthodox research into the type of death Jesus suffered in his crucifixion. Using cadavers, he demonstrated that the nails must have been driven through the wrists and not the hands, because the hands didn't have enough muscle tissue to support the weight of a mature male body. He went on to describe the excruciating agony of such an impalement that would have pierced a junction of three major nerves. He also showed that death was eventually caused by suffocation when the victim could no longer push himself up on the spike through the feet to draw air into the lungs.

Moved by this graphic description of how Jesus suffered, I asked our pastor if I could share what I'd read with the congregation at the Good Friday service. He agreed and in my first attempt ever at public speaking I shared from my heart what Jesus had endured on the cross. Although I was very impassioned, I realized later that I was still missing a vital piece of understanding. I did not have the revelation yet that He had suffered all this in my place. It was not yet personal for me.

Mo watched my new and intense pursuit of spiritual truths with mixed feelings. Since she hadn't experienced what I did in the bar, she couldn't quite figure out what I was trying to accomplish. I'd follow her around the house reading different passages from books I thought were particularly insightful only to see her go off shaking her head wondering how much longer this was going to continue.

Undaunted, I continued my quest. In church each Sunday I became far more attentive in order to pick up any morsel of truth I could. I started taking communion more regularly and more seriously. I added a litany of religious activities to my daily routine such as saying the rosary as I drove to work, using the ten holes on my steering wheel as the beads. I also took to wearing a brown scapular blessed by a priest. Although I was never quite sure what it did for me, I figured it couldn't hurt. I then added a Miraculous Medal on a neck chain to my spiritual armament. Church tradition taught it had been designed by the Virgin Mary herself, thereby conferring extraordinary graces to the wearer. And for good measure, I would light a votive candle in church on occasion as a flickering petition to let God know I was here and desperately trying to get His attention.

I also started collecting the short, little one-sentence prayer cards from the back of the church that promised a certain amount of time off in Purgatory with each reading. If I found one that knocked off a hundred years of torment, I'd discard one of the lesser petitions that gave me only, say, a month's reduction. I started collecting them like coupons. I just hoped someone in heaven's general accounting was keeping track of all my earned time off. One day, I had the disquieting thought that if I could knock off a hundred years in Purgatory with one prayer and seemingly make only a dent in my sentence, just how long was I actually going to be in there? I decided not to think about that too long, but to just stick to my regimen.

In addition to all these appeals to God I included a booklet of prayers from St. Bridgett. This Swedish saint claimed she had been told by an angel, that if anyone prayed these prayers faithfully every day for a year, that Jesus, Mary, and Joseph would meet them at their deathbed and personally escort them into heaven. Here at last was a way to avoid purgatory altogether and I went for it. So every night I knelt by my bed for forty-five minutes, drunk or sober, and prayed those prayers. Three months into it I missed a night and I had to start over, so it took me a total of 15 months to finish it. But I did it.

As the year progressed I continued to employ almost every means made available to me in the Catholic Church to please God and learn more about Him. And even though I thought all this activity was bringing me closer to knowing God, in reality I was still taking everybody else's word about Him. It was obvious many great men and women knew Him, or seemed to, but the fact was, I still had no more personal, first-hand knowledge of God then when I started.

But God was about to change that in a hurry.

Chapter 2

The First Encounter

At a party one evening, Mo and I and got talking to some old friends we hadn't seen in awhile. They told us they had just come back from a weekend experience called a Marriage Encounter. They were both very excited as they related how this 'encounter' had re-ignited the love in their marriage. They explained that Marriage Encounter wasn't for problem marriages, although it couldn't hurt, but was designed to make a good marriage better. It was like getting "a marriage tune-up."

Beyond that, however, they were reluctant to give us too much information, saying it was better if we just went and experienced it for ourselves. It sounded a little weird to me, but there was no denying that something good had happened to them. They were so certain we would love it they offered to watch our kids if we would just go on one. Who can turn down an offer like that? So we agreed to sign up for the next one, which we found out was in about a month. I figured it would be okay to put my heavenly investigation on hold for a couple of days in order to spend some quality time working on my marriage.

Mo and I had been married eight years at this point, and had three small children. As good Catholics, who thought birth control was a Protestant doctrine, we had wasted no time getting pregnant. Within a year we had a beautiful little girl named Tara. Twelve months later God sent us our first-born son, Christopher, who arrived with a mop of blond hair and big round eyes. Brendan, our always active second son, followed three years after that.

As our family grew, and my career advanced, we kept moving up the ladder to bigger and better houses. We had just moved into our third one, a large four-bedroom rancher on an acre with a pool in north Stamford, Connecticut, which we had bought from my parents. My mother, who had recently separated from my father, could no longer operate the big house by herself and put it up for sale. When it didn't sell after a year, and the listing ran out, we realized suddenly we could afford it and purchased it from her.

I felt my marriage to Mo was as good as any marriage could be. Right from the start we felt we were made for each other. We had both grown up on Long Island, although in very different communities. She lived in a small Cape Cod in Bellmore, a rural community in Nassau County on the south side of the Island. While my folks lived on the north side, closer to Manhattan, in a six-story brick apartment building in Jackson Heights, Queens. As God would have it, both our families eventually moved to Greenwich, Connecticut and Mo and I ended up at the same Catholic high school, St Mary's. But I was four years older and had already graduated when she arrived, so we didn't actually meet until I was in college.

The only reason we did meet was because my brother Neil was dating her best friend, Pat, who he later married. So whenever Pat came by the house, she was usually accompanied by Mo and her boyfriend. I didn't pay much attention to them at the time since they were just my kid brother's high school friends. But I must have started to notice her. I remember sitting in a pub a year or two later drinking beers with friends from high school, when one of my pals announced he was getting married. He was the first in our group to take that step. I was shocked, since for me marriage was still a word that belonged to my parent's generation, not mine. I joked that I was not likely to consider marriage for a long time, if ever, and if I did get hooked up it would only be with Mo Torpey. And since she already had a pretty serious boyfriend, that was not very likely.

Although I felt safe and secure behind my beer-soaked analysis, I was startled by my confession. When did Mo Torpey become the love of my life? We hadn't ever dated or expressed one word of interest in each other.

When I finally moved out of my parent's house and got my own apartment in Greenwich Village in Manhattan, I didn't see Mo as much anymore. However, there was one person who reported to me regularly about her whereabouts and activities: my mother. She knew a genuine person and potential wife for her son when she saw her and she wasn't about to let her get out of my sight. So when her boyfriend broke up with her, I was probably the next person on the planet to learn of it.

It wasn't long before we were dating. I had gotten into skiing, and that winter I introduced her to the sport. We'd go up to the Wyndham ski area in the Catskills each weekend with a bunch of my friends and their girlfriends and have a wonderful time. I always felt comfortable being with Mo. I never had to scramble for something to say to keep the conversation alive. We just hit it off right from the start. As our dating increased I felt my whole world starting to revolve more and more around this beautiful blond-haired girl with the laughing blue eyes. However love happens, it was definitely happening to me.

As for Mo, she told me she always sort of had an eye on me. But because she was already dating, and considered herself a loyal gal, she didn't let her heart go astray. The first time the gong rang for her was when my brother picked me up at the train station one evening, and she and Pat and her boyfriend went along for the ride. When she saw me standing at the station all decked out in a suit and tie, holding a briefcase and sporting a green Fedora (which made that hat the best ten-dollar investment of my life), she thought, "He's not like all the boys I know. He's actually a man with a real job." Fortunately for me, she didn't know how insecure and un-manlike that 23-year-old really was beneath all that garb.

For me, I think the clincher came after we started dating and I brought her into the city for an office party held at my boss's apartment. Since these folks were older and pretty sophisticated New Yorkers, I wasn't sure how she was going to handle them. No problem. She waded in among them shaking hands, asking them questions about themselves, piecing all the names I'd mentioned with the faces and generally relating to them like old friends. They all loved her. I was blown away at how mature and self-confident she was. And the lingering image I think I still had of her being a young, hometown girlfriend went out the window. I realized Mo was truly a woman who was more than capable of holding her own in this world.

But it took a bold move by my mother to actually bring me face to face with the "M" word. We'd been dating less than a year, and I was still in the "going steady" mindset that I suspect a lot of guys my age fell into back in that day. However, on a weekend visit home to my parent's house, as I was about to go out the door on a date with Mo, my mother suddenly confronted me with a question only a mother could ask, "So Brian, when are you going to declare your intentions to Mo?"

Declare my intentions? Although I laughed at my mother's antiquated phrasing, she definitely got through to me. With a big gulp in my throat, I suddenly realized this was not like high school and college where you dated just for the sake of dating. This time it was for keeps. And I decided right then and there Mo was a keeper. A few weeks later I purchased a ring with the help of my father who knew a guy who knew a guy, and in the spring of 1966 I asked Mo to marry me.

Now, eight years and three kids later I considered it one of the smartest moves I had ever made. But as good as I thought our marriage was, it was about to get a whole lot better.

The Marriage Encounter weekend we signed up for was being held at an Episcopal retreat center in upstate Connecticut. It was billed as an inter-denominational gathering, and some twenty couples had showed up looking every bit as nervous and uncertain about this weekend as we were.

Although a Catholic priest was present to act as a counselor, the weekend was really run by a few volunteer married host couples. At each session one of these couples would share openly from their personal lives, emphasizing how they felt about each life incident they described. Some of their stories were pretty hilarious. Like the guy who shared how he could put a full-course breakfast on the table in no time flat. And how he assumed his lovely new bride had received the same life-training course he had. So on the first morning of their marriage, after showering and shaving, he came downstairs expecting to be greeted by a complete, mouth-watering breakfast. Instead, he found his wife in tears trying to figure out how to work the toaster. He said it was funny now, but not then. A marriage encounter had helped him finally accept his wife's shortcomings and deal with the negative feelings they engendered in him. And to realize he wasn't Mr. Perfect, either.

Feelings, we were taught, are neither right nor wrong. They have no moral value whatsoever. They are just programmed emotional responses to present situations that we learned through our childhood experiences. If somebody with red hair bullied you as a kid, you could have an uncomfortable feeling being around someone with red hair. Feelings are so closely identified with who we are as a person, it takes courage to actually verbalize them and risk being rejected.

After each session Mo and I would go off, as instructed, and write privately for ten minutes in our notebook about a particular topic, like, "how do I feel on a cloudy day?" We'd then switch notebooks, read what the other had written, and discuss it. Little by little, Mo and I began to open up to each other in new and deeper ways. Like most men, I tended to bury my feelings, fearful that they might signal a weakness. It felt good to just let it all out and see that my feelings were accepted. With each sharing I felt lighter—and more connected to Mo.

Although this was not supposed to be a religious weekend, there were posters around that informed us God was watching and people were praying for us. It was reassuring to know that I hadn't totally left the spiritual realm while I was working on my marriage. One poster in particular caught my eye. It read, "If you don't feel close to God, who moved?" That really made me stop and think.

After the last session on Saturday evening, all the couples were gathered together to hear a candlelight reading from the Bible about the Marriage Feast of Cana where Jesus turned the water into wine. It was like a big group hug that sent us all to our rooms for the night feeling everything was under control.

Later, as Mo and I were dozing off to sleep, exhausted from the day's emotional workout, she suddenly exclaimed to no one in particular, "Oh, I feel God is here." And then promptly closed her eyes and fell asleep. I lay there a while longer thinking about her puzzling remark and reflecting on the new love I felt for her as a result of all our sharing. That's when I noticed the shaft of hall light coming into our room through the transom over the door.

As I studied the beam, it suddenly grew and overwhelmed all my senses. Wave after wave of liquid love began to wash over me, down to my very soul. I knew somehow that I was in the presence of God, my heavenly Father, who loved me intimately. He began speaking to me. Telling me that I had been uniquely handcrafted by Him in my mother's womb. That there was nothing about my whole being that was accidental. That every part of my physical body and personality had been designed by Him for a specific purpose. And that He had called me to this purpose from eternity. I learned all this before I ever read the 139th Psalm, which reiterates the very message God spoke to me that night.

In the midst of this revelation, a scene appeared. I saw ranks of men in white robes moving steadily forward in a triangular shaped phalanx. First one, then two, then three, and so forth. They didn't seem to be walking, but gliding forth as one body. It reminded me of the ending of an old John Wayne war movie I'd seen where the all the soldiers who had been killed floated over the last scene as the victorious army marched away after the battle.

I understood that this was the army of God and that I was being recruited. Even more, that I would become a leader in this army. I was amazed, since I had always been more of a follower than a leader. One of the Scriptures I found later that I feel best captures the spirit of this vision is Psalm 110, verse 3: *"Your troops will be willing on your day of battle. Arrayed in holy majesty, from the womb of the dawn, you will receive the dew of your youth."*

In that moment of time, I have no idea how long it lasted, a lifetime of insecurity and fear melted away like a snowball in summer. I realized I had finally met my Maker. And that He knew me and loved me and had chosen me. My life suddenly was filled with new meaning and purpose.

I awoke the next morning with love in my heart for all creation. I loved God. I loved my wife. I loved everyone in the world—even the unlovely and the unlikable. As the Bible says, *"We (can) love, because He first loved us"* (1 John 4:19). I realized I would never have to measure myself against another person again. It was a practice that usually left me feeling inferior because I felt I had so many shortcomings. I now knew I was unique. Not better or worse, just unique. As all men are. I wanted to tell all the hurting people in the world that it's okay to come out from behind their masks. It's okay. God is real. And He loves us!

When I went outside that morning, it seemed like all creation was worshipping God. All the trees and shrubs, especially the rhododendron, seemed to have their leaves and branches upraised and praising the One who created us all. It was a wondrous time.

Later I would read in the Bible, *"You will seek me and find me when you seek me with all your heart"* (Jer. 29:13). I had been searching with all my heart (a search He Himself had provoked), and true to His word—I'd found Him. Or rather He had found me. It was the beginning of my appreciation of the total sovereignty of God—even over Satan. That He is a hands-on, micro-manager who is totally in control of every thing, every person and every event under heaven. That, *"In Him we were also chosen, having been predestined according to the plan of him who works out everything in conformity with the purpose of His will"* (Ephesians 1:11).

    My experience was so profound, I was even reluctant to tell Mo that first day for fear she wouldn't believe me. But finally I did, only to discover that she too had experienced a divine touch during the night. Probably right after she exclaimed about "God being here." She had no trouble accepting my whole experience, or I hers. I will always be thankful to the Lord that He started us off on the same page. In the days and months ahead we would need to draw on each other's faith and support more and more.

    Although I wouldn't hear the biblical term "born again" for another year and a half, I believe that was exactly what I experienced. For Mo, as we later discovered, it was more of a renewal. It seems she had a real spiritual awakening to the reality of Christ as a teenager while on a girl's retreat. She just never received the necessary spiritual teaching afterwards to explain the new birth to her and how to walk in it. And at this point in our story, we were both totally clueless when it came to spiritual understanding. But we were waking up.

Chapter 3
Adjusting to New Realities

Now that we had this real relationship with God, Mo and I naturally assumed it should be continued through greater participation in our local church. So overnight, we became the most active members at our Catholic church. Every time they opened the doors, Mo and I and the kids would be there. Even on the feast days of minor saints, when only a handful of older folks showed up, we'd arrive dressed up and smiling. We wanted everyone in the church to know that we had finally caught up with them and were now on board with the whole thing. You see, we just assumed that everyone there already knew God and had been patiently waiting for us to get with the program. We actually felt a little embarrassed for being clueless for so long.

As we attempted to smile our way into the hearts of our fellow parishioners, we also determined to get to know our pastor better. Father Sal, as he was known, was the only priest assigned to the parish. Assisting him in his duties was a handful of nuns who taught at the school and who cloistered themselves in a convent on the property. Father Sal lived completely alone in a large house nearby, without even a caretaker for company. He seemed to prefer it that way. He was definitely not a warm fuzzy person. We'd heard how he had rankled several members of the congregation with the autocratic way he dealt with problems that arose. In his mind, this was his parish, and he made sure everyone knew that. As a result, he was not well liked. So we took him on as a challenge. We decided all he needed was for someone to show him some unconditional love and he'd warm right up.

One winter's day, for example, we noticed his log pile was getting low. So I left notes on all the car windshields to bring a log to church the following Sunday. Many did and Father Sal ended up with a cord of wood in the parking lot. But it didn't seem to have much effect on him. When he found out who organized it, he told me he didn't really need the wood. I guess he had more in the basement or somewhere. I forget if he ever said thank you or not.

To show him how much we cared about the parish, I volunteered to act as co-chairman for the big annual fund raiser in the church. Called a Las Vegas Night, it was held in the school cafeteria, which became the church sanctuary on Sunday. Gaming tables were brought in with professionals to run them, and a bar was set up where the pulpit normally would be on Sunday. The whole time I was organizing it I kept having these queasy feelings, but told myself it must be alright—Father Sal had okayed it. I personally spray painted some one thousand poker chips, gold, silver and bronze in my basement for the event. Looking back, I shudder at how naive I was.

Besides church life, my new awakening to God was also having an effect on how I approached my job. I always assumed that my ability to come up with good advertising ideas was due to having some special ad gene in my DNA. But now I realized that God was in charge of all that happened in this universe, big and small. Which meant it was God giving me those ideas all along.

My immediate reaction to this new understanding was to feel a bit deflated. You mean I'm just a conduit? A mailbox in which God places the ideas and I merely extract them? It made me feel a little useless until I considered who it was giving me these wonderful concepts—God Almighty! How awesome was that? From then on I just began to praise Him and thank Him for doing that for me. One of the immediate benefits was a reduction in stress since I now realized it was not dependent upon me to come up with the idea. Oh, I had to do my due diligence, but knowing it was God who would "mail" it to me in His perfect timing, I simply included prayer as part of that due diligence. It was a very exciting new way to do advertising.

That wasn't the only exciting change in my life that year. In March, our fourth child, Todd, shoved his broad shoulders into the world to join the family.

If we didn't have enough going on, Mo and I decided to stay involved with Marriage Encounter by joining a follow-up program. We'd meet monthly in different homes with other Encounter graduates in the area to keep the fire going. Those times of sharing became a great source of fellowship and growth for us as we continued to try and sort out all that had happened to us.

Because we encountered God on our weekend experience, we thought it was a great way for everyone to meet God. So we became Marriage Encounter evangelists. We encouraged everyone we loved and cared for to go on a weekend. My brother Neil and his wife Pat, Mo's sister, Kathy and her husband Jerry, and Mo's parents all trusted us enough to go on a weekend. Not only family, but good friends like our next-door neighbors from Old Greenwich, Bob and Mary Anne Morelli, also went. And although they all experienced wonderful renewals in their marriages, none seemed to have the "God experience" we did. That puzzled us at first. It took us awhile to realize that what we experienced was truly unique. (We did hear later of two other couples who also had a God-encounter on their weekend, but for most it was just a great marriage renewal experience.)

We were also waking up to another misconception we had labored under, which was that our fellow parishioners were spiritually ahead of us. The truth was, we had actually experienced something they had not. This became apparent whenever we'd share our experience with a church member and see their puzzled reactions. They'd mumble something like, "That's nice," or, "I'm glad for you," and then walk off. It was obvious they had no idea what we were talking about. Some even seemed to fear us. Consequently, we felt a certain distancing come between us and them no matter how hard we tried to unite with them. Even Father Sal at one point asked us, with more than a hint of annoyance, "Where'd you get your faith?"

As the year progressed I began to grow discouraged. I had thought that the more involved we became in our church, the more of the life of God we'd experience. But it wasn't happening. Aside from our Marriage Encounter involvement, the one other source of spiritual nourishment I found, oddly enough, was in the earthy, soul-stirring lyrics of John Denver's music. His mystical campfire song, Rocky Mountain High, which spoke of being "born again," strangely resonated in my spirit without me even knowing the Biblical truth it was confirming. The same with Annie's Song. When he crooned, *"you fill up my senses, like a night in a forest ...come fill me again,"* I sang along like it was a prayer expressing the deepest cry of my heart.

For almost a year I carried the smoldering afterglow of my God encounter deep within. But I could feel the warmth of the embers fading with each passing month. I desperately needed a recharge. I was afraid if I didn't get one soon that not even John Denver's plaintive tunes would be able to fan the flame back to life.

Frustrated by our inability to touch God again at His official place of residence, as we continued to see the church at that time, Mo and I decided to go on another Marriage Encounter. This still was the only venue where we'd actually met God. We desperately hoped we'd find Him there again.

This second Marriage Encounter took place in a different facility in a different part of the state. But once again it was an interdenominational gathering with a Catholic priest acting as the spiritual advisor. And once again God paid us—or rather Mo—a visit on Saturday night.

As we completed the last session on Saturday, Mo began to sense a conflict developing within herself. She didn't say anything about it until we returned to our room for the evening. She said she felt like something inside her wanted to come out, but there was a block. So while I stayed in the room and got ready for God, since this was the time He'd visited us before, Mo decided to go and talk to the priest about her problem.

I must have fallen asleep because I didn't remember Mo coming back into room. The next morning when we awoke she told me the cork had popped out last night and she was free. She definitely looked different—more peaceful—but she was reluctant to tell me anything more about it at that time. I on the other hand was quite downhearted, since the night had come and gone and I'd not heard a word from heaven. When I told Mo of my disappointment at not receiving another touch from God, she just smiled confidently and said, "Don't worry, Hon, He's here. You'll see. Just don't be too anxious, and it will happen."

Since it was Sunday morning we headed downstairs to a room off the lobby where a small group of Catholics had gathered for a communion service. The priest, the same one Mo had talked to the night before, had offered to perform a Mass for those who wanted to gather early. I'd never attended a Mass in such an intimate, informal setting before and I liked the feeling. The priest even shared a little joke with us that had a powerful effect on me.

The joke was about St. Peter giving a tour in heaven. After showing them the wonders of the pearly gates and the streets of gold, the group suddenly came upon a high wall. St. Peter asked the group to quiet their voices as they passed by the wall. "Why?" asked one person in the group. "Well," said St. Peter, "behind that wall are the Catholics. And they think they are the only ones up here."

In that moment I realized how absurd it was to think that only Catholics went to heaven. Yet that had been my lifetime belief, nurtured no doubt by sixteen years of Catholic education that had stressed that very point. But with one joke, this honest priest had demolished that false belief in me forever. It was the first step in what would soon become a rush for freedom.

As I settled in for the final session of the weekend, still with no sign of God, I started to think about the unthinkable. What if God didn't show up? What would I do then? Where else could I go to find Him? I could feel desperation begin to trickle through my sweat glands. Then suddenly I sensed something. The curtains in front of the open window stirred softly. I became instantly aware of a gentle, but persistent breeze blowing in the trees. My heart pounded. It was Him! He'd come! But just as quickly as the wind started, it quieted. Puzzled, but strangely encouraged, I returned my attention to the story the host couple was sharing.

Instead of a personal story, this couple had elected to play a tape narrating the story of a bunny named Barrington from a book called <u>The Way of the Wolf</u>. As the only rabbit in the forest, Barrington is extremely lonely and feels like he doesn't fit in. One day a grey wolf approaches him and tells him he is very gifted, so he shouldn't despair. He tells him all the animals in the forest are his family. Since it is Christmas Eve, Barrington decides to leave a free gift outside the home of each one of the animals to express his new-found love for them. After completing his secret mission, the weather suddenly turns colder and begins to snow. Hurrying home, Barrington spots a little mouse that is lost and shelters him under his warm fur throughout the frigid night. In the morning, the mouse is alive but Barrington has died. His carcass lies unnoticed on the forest floor except by the grey wolf, which comes and stands over him all Christmas day until night falls. Then the wolf leaves and returns to the forest.

The wolf clearly represented God to me, who sees all and knows all. And I could sure relate to Barrington Bunny.

I returned to our room to write about how the story made me feel. (For some reason, Mo went to another location.) But I was now in such an emotional state that I couldn't write a thing. Suddenly all the frustrations of the previous year, plus the fear of not finding God on the weekend, overwhelmed me. I collapsed upon the bed with deep, gut-wrenching sobs that grew in intensity. A lifetime accumulation of humiliations, disappointments, fears and rejections suddenly came gushing out of me. But as my emotional basket emptied I sensed a sweet change taking place within. A warm joy began to bubble up from the depth of my belly, replacing all the hurt and disappointment and filling me with peace and well being. And then I heard a small, still voice float quietly into my mind, and whisper, *"I will never leave you or forsake you."*

I suddenly realized God was inside me now—in my spirit. And not out in space somewhere. Or in a church building. I realized I never had to be afraid again that He'd go off to some unapproachable place in the sky where I couldn't find Him. Geography would never distance Him from me again. We were now inseparable! The flame of His presence would never go out.

Later, Mo finally told me what happened the night when she visited the priest. Unknown to me, she'd been carrying around in her soul a painful incident that had happened to her some fifteen years earlier as a teenager. She had been sexually molested by her father. The incident, and there was only one, was severe enough to cause a suffocating wedge of unforgiveness to lodge in her spirit and block God's love from flowing through her. In forgiving him that night she had been gloriously set free and filled with God's Spirit. The "cork" of unforgiveness was permanently removed. Later she wrote her father a letter to let him know that she had forgiven him. And the two were later reconciled when he had his own encounter with God.

I believe we were both filled with the Holy Spirit on that weekend. But because we had no one to instruct us, and because we had not yet started to read the Bible for ourselves, we remained ignorant of these spiritual truths. It still amazes me that I never once thought to take Bob Vogel's advice and pick up the Bible and read it. As Catholics, the Bible was uncharted territory.

But we were about to get some guidance that would take us to new frontiers!

Chapter 4

Tongues of Fire

About a month after returning from this second God encounter, we received three paperback books anonymously in the mail one day: <u>Cross and the Switchblade</u>, by David Wilkerson; <u>They Speak in Other Tongues</u>, by John Sherrill; and another one about a Catholic charismatic church in Providence, R.I. We had not heard anything about the Charismatic Movement before, which takes its name from the Greek word *charisma,* meaning "a gift of grace," and wondered who would have sent the books to us. (We never did find out.) But those three books changed our lives. They were exactly what we needed to take the next step in our spiritual awakening.

All three books told stories of Christians from different denominations that had experienced something called the baptism of the Holy Spirit. This experience imparted a number of supernatural abilities to the believer, the most controversial one being the gift of tongues. It seems the first time this phenomenon took place was right after the ascension of Jesus into heaven, as told in the second chapter of the Book of Acts. Jesus had told His apostles not to do anything but to wait in Jerusalem until they had received *"what the Father had promised"* (Acts 1:4. NAS). They probably had no idea what Jesus was talking about, but waited anyway. Nine days passed and nothing happened. Then on the tenth day, the Feast of Pentecost, the Jewish feast that came fifty days after Passover, the building where they were waiting and praying was rocked by a mighty rushing wind. *"And they were all filled with the Holy Spirit and began to speak with other tongues, as the Spirit was giving them utterance"* (Acts 2:4, NAS).

Mo was so moved by the stories of these modern-day manifestations of the experience she wanted to rush down to Brooklyn where several of these groups were reportedly located, so she could see for herself. It all sounded so mysterious and exciting.

Since the Charismatic Movement had an expression in the Catholic Church, we plunged right into it. Or at least we tried to. Even though the books indicated that any Christian could pray with any other believer wanting to receive this experience, in the Catholic Church it had already been systematized into a seven-week Life in the Spirit seminar. And the next seminar in our area, we discovered, wasn't scheduled for another month. However, we were told one had just gotten underway in a church in Westport that we could jump into if we wanted. We signed up immediately.

When we arrived the first evening, we were handed a little booklet that explained the scriptural justification for this experience. It also outlined the nine different supernatural manifestations of the Holy Spirit, or "gifts" for ministry, that we could experience after being prayed for. All these giftings are listed and discussed in the Bible in 1 Corinthians, chapters 12 and 14. The gifts fell into three categories: thought, word and deed. The three thought gifts were a word of knowledge (a revelation of facts about someone or some situation), wisdom (insight to know what to do) and discernment of evil spirits. The three word gifts were speaking in an unknown language or tongue (both as a personal prayer language and a public utterance), the gift of interpreting a publicly spoken unknown tongue, and prophecy. And the three deed, or action, gifts were miracles, healing and faith. We wanted to experience the whole enchilada.

The class, which included a number of non-Catholics, was led by the pastor of the church where it was being held. He was informative, but boring. We told ourselves to be patient, because when the seminar concluded they would lay hands on us and pray that we receive this infilling of the Holy Spirit. That's when it would get very exciting.

The second week was no better than the first, except at the conclusion of this session the pastor announced a communion service would take place and invited us all to partake. We couldn't believe what happened next. An altar boy came forward with two chalices, one of silver and one of gold, and handed them to the pastor. Turning to the group, this priest explained that the Catholics present would be served from the gold chalice and Protestants from the silver one. This was because only Catholics could receive communion blessed by a priest. He then instructed the Catholics to form one line and the Protestants another. We expected all the Protestants to start heading for the door rather than subject themselves to this humiliating second class treatment. Instead, we were stunned when a number of them actually got up and formed a line leading up to the silver chalice. We were so uncomfortable with the whole thing we remained seated and did not participate.

Afterwards we approached the pastor and questioned him about his behavior. "Everything we have read about the Charismatic Movement," I told him, "indicates that one of the main reasons God is pouring out His Spirit on the church today is to unify us in Him. But it seems what you did, divides us again."

"I'm glad you noticed that," he said, fixing me with a smile that showed great patience for my naiveté. "We always want to remind our 'separated brethren,'" a term Catholic clergy used when referring to Protestants, "that there is a greater benefit to being Catholic so they become jealous and want to rejoin the fold."

Mo and I just stared at him, realizing this man had no interest whatsoever in the spiritual growth each believer would receive from the Baptism of the Holy Spirit. Rather he saw this whole seminar simply as an opportunity for recruitment. We never went back.

We were now forced to wait for the next regularly scheduled seminar, which was still two weeks away. This one would take place at the Bishop's church in Bridgeport, the head church in the diocese. We signed up for it.

When it finally started, we found it more to our liking. The priests and nuns and lay people attending were more loving and had a real joy and excitement about them. We felt the leadership had genuinely experienced the Spirit baptism and we cruised through the seven weeks. In addition to the teaching, each session began with a prayer meeting where we heard people praying in tongues for the first time. I remember feeling a tingling expectancy at those meetings that God was about to show up at any minute. Either in a word of prophecy. Or a tongue. Or an interpretation of tongues. It was very exciting. Mo and I were like wide-eyed kids in a candy store. It was during a time of singing a song about Jesus in one of those meetings that that still, small voice whispered to me again, and said: *"I am alive!"* The reality of the resurrection of Jesus hit me like a sledgehammer. He really had risen—and He was alive! Right here! Today!

Reading the seminar booklet they handed out at these meetings, I finally found the Scriptural words that explained what happened to us spiritually on our first marriage encounter. And they were from the Old Testament, not the New.

The words were spoken by the prophet Ezekiel, almost 600 years before Jesus: *"Moreover, I will give you a new heart, and put a new spirit within you; and I will remove the heart of stone out of your flesh and give you a heart of flesh. And I will put My Spirit within you, and cause you to walk in My statutes, and you will be careful to observe My ordinances"* (Ezek. 36:26, 27, NAS).

I showed the verse to Mo and we both finally understood our experience hadn't been a fluke thing that we had experienced, rather, it was the fulfillment of a promise made over 2600 years ago to all of God's chosen people. It was the same promise that Jesus said would be fulfilled in those who believed in Him when He declared, *"I tell you the truth, no one can see the kingdom of God unless he is born again"* (John 3: 3). Even though we hadn't been looking for a "new heart," it was God's sovereign grace and good pleasure to give it to us in His perfect timing.

Looking back on those Catholic Life in the Spirit seminars, we realized that the new birth was never really taught or emphasized as a preliminary necessity. How could it be when the church taught we were birthed into the Kingdom by our water baptism? Like us, I'm sure many of those Catholics did have a genuine born again experience even if they were ignorant of what had happened to them. But I also suspect many did not.

After the final class, it was finally time for us to be prayed for the baptism of the Holy Spirit. Several men and women gathered around each candidate. After placing their hands on our heads and shoulders and arms, they began asking Jesus to fill us with the Holy Spirit. Mo started speaking in an unknown tongue right away, signifying she had received. But I was having trouble. I probably would have spoken in tongues, except that a woman who was praying for me was painfully pressing some sort of medal into my palm. And all I could think was, dear Jesus, if she didn't stop soon, the image on that medal was going to be with me forever. I finally did get my prayer language, but it was many months later.

Even though I believe we received the infilling of the Spirit on that second marriage encounter, this experience made it official for both of us. And by going through the process, Mo received the gift of tongues.

Following this seminar, we were also now convinced that all spiritual truth is based solely on what is revealed in the Bible. It is, as one preacher put it, "the truth, the whole truth and nothing but the truth." Remembering I still had my old Catholic Douay-Rheims Bible from high school, I went and dug it out of the closet. I couldn't believe I'd hung onto it all these years. It had been my Junior-year textbook for a half-semester course on the Old Testament. But all we ever studied was Leviticus, Numbers and Deuteronomy. It was so boring I hadn't opened it since. Which is probably why I never thought about reading the Bible at any time during my search for God.

Since Mo didn't have a Bible, she went out and purchased a new one. She came home with the Living Bible, a conversational translation that leaves out all the "thees" and "thous" and gives it to you in plain English.

From then on, the Bible became our best friend and resource. Oh, how many times I wished I had taken Bob Vogel's advice and started to read the Bible from day one. It would have saved me a lot of searching in all the wrong the places. But I guess the Lord wanted me to dig down to the bottom of my religion to discover that there was nothing there. That way, no one could ever say you didn't try this or that. I tried it all—and came up empty. But at this point in our story we still hadn't gotten to the bottom yet.

With the baptism of the Holy Spirit we now had something to give people to help them connect with God. So, just as we beat the drum for Marriage Encounter, we did the same for this experience. Pretty soon we were praying for everyone we could. We told them they didn't need to take a seven-week, Life-In-The-Spirit Seminar like we did. We just showed them the verses in the Bible, explained what they meant, and asked if they wanted to receive it. If they said yes, we prayed for them.

But first we told them that before they could receive this "second blessing" they first needed to be born again. Most of the folks we prayed for were Catholics, so they already believed in the historical Jesus. But most had not yet taken that personal step of commitment and invited Him into their hearts as Savior. For those who believed they already had, we pointed out that a person can be born again but still not have received the baptism of the Holy Spirit. For some reason God did not permanently link the two experiences together. Sometimes you got both at once, sometimes not. But without this second experience you won't have the supernatural power needed to live the Christian life. We see that revealed in Acts 19 where Paul encounters some disciples in Ephesus and notices something amiss. So he asks them, *"Did you receive the Holy Spirit when you believed?"* It turned out they had not. So when he laid hands on them *"the Holy Spirit came on them, and they began speaking with other tongues and prophesying"* (Acts 19:2-6, NAS).

Since the Spirit baptism isn't automatically connected to being born again, it's easy to see how it could have gotten separated over the centuries and simply forgotten. And it would have stayed forgotten were it not for a handful of Spirit-prompted believers in the early 1900's who saw in the Scriptures this phenomenon of praying in tongues and earnestly sought God to receive it. That led to the great Azusa Street revival in Los Angeles when the Holy Spirit was again poured out on believers in large public demonstrations of power and glory. It then quickly spread around the world and resulted in many Spirit-baptized believers being expelled from their churches by prelates who were frightened by the supernatural manifestations that accompanied this experience. These ousted believers, who did not understand that God was setting them free from all institutional religion, eventually reformed themselves into congregations known as the Pentecostal churches. Today, many of these churches, which were once on the cutting edge of Christianity, are as powerless as the churches they once left.

The charismatic renewal, which hit in the '60's and lasted through the '70's, seems to have been the second wave of the Pentecostal Movement. It swept through the mainline denominations, and especially through the sacramental churches—the Catholic, Lutheran and Episcopal, which had largely been overlooked in the earlier outpouring. It was as if God was backtracking a bit to make sure all His people who were hidden away in these places got a chance to receive this second blessing, too.

So Mo and I started doing our part to spread the word as we offered to pray for family members and friends who wanted more of God. And sure enough, they all started receiving this Spirit baptism, including the gift of speaking in tongues.

I remember my brother Neil's experience especially. He and Pat were closely following our spiritual journey and were open to all that we shared with them. On the way home after one of our conversations, Pat turned to Neil and said, "I believe all that Mo and Brian are saying is true. They wouldn't lie to us." And she rolled down the window and threw out her cigarettes as a sign of her belief and willingness to go after all that God had for her. Later, she and Neil asked us to pray for them for the Holy Spirit baptism and we did. I don't remember what happened with Pat, but Neil immediately began jabbering away in his new tongue and sobbing and saying to God, "I can't believe You would do this for *me*."

We also prayed for our older children, Tara and Chris, who were now nine and eight respectively. They too received it and immediately began praying with childlike innocence in their new heavenly prayer language.

My 72 year-old mother was another exciting story. She had seen the changes in our lives resulting from the baptism of the Holy Spirit, especially the joy, and she wanted to experience this blessing also. Mom had been a faithful Catholic her whole life who loved God and who would attend mass almost every morning in her attempt to be near Him. But she now knew there was something more and she was honest enough at her age to admit she didn't have whatever it was.

We explained to her about the necessity of first accepting Jesus as her savior, before we prayed for the Holy Spirit.

"But I've always believed in Jesus," she answered. "We know Mom," we replied, "but we've discovered we need to do more than just believe Jesus lived and died on a cross and rose again. The Bible says that even the devil believes in Jesus, but he sure doesn't accept Him as his savior. We also need to believe He took the punishment for all our sins so we could be completely forgiven by God and assured of heaven. And unfortunately, as Catholics, we were never told to take the next step and *receive* His forgiveness by faith and stop trying to earn it on our own with good works."

Mom had no problem with that and humbly bowed her head and invited Jesus into her heart. It's possible she had already been born again, but we just wanted to make sure. When she had done that, Mo and I then placed our hands on her head and asked Jesus to fill her with His Holy Spirit. We prayed for several minutes over her, but nothing happened that we could tell. We told her not to worry; it sometimes kicks in later, especially at night when your mind is at rest. We'd learned that the logical mind often gets in the way as it tries to rationalize the whole thing. But several days went by and there was no change in her.

Then Mo had what could only be described as a divine insight. She asked Mom if she had ever forgiven my father for his drinking and infidelity, which had been the cause of their separation. She replied that she had.

"But have you ever told him?" Mo pressed. When Mom answered, "no, I don't think so," Mo suggested she write him a letter and let him know he was forgiven. She said she would.

The next morning the phone rang. It was my mother, all excited, telling us she wrote the letter to my father and then went to bed. However, around midnight she was awakened by the sensation of water being poured all over her. Suddenly she was swimming in the love of God, she said, and began crying and speaking in tongues and praising God. She didn't know how to stop it, so she continued doing that for a couple of hours before drifting off to sleep again. She just had to call and tell us she finally had the joy she so desperately wanted.

BAPTISM

Brian Hennessy

The more we read our Bibles and the stirring testimony books about what God was doing in the lives of ordinary men and women across the denominational spectrum, the more our understanding of spiritual truths grew.

This awakening took a quantum leap when we began attending a Bible study at an Episcopal Church about a twenty minute drive from our house. Someone had told Mo, "If you want to experience a real on-fire charismatic church, visit St. Pauls."

After locating the church in Darien, just off the Merritt Parkway, Mo started attending Tuesday morning Bible studies. She found the teaching there so good that she convinced me to go to the men's Bible study on Wednesday evenings.

The study was taught by a priest they called "Terry," who was the head pastor—or rector, as that office is called in the Episcopal Church. Just addressing a priest without the title of "Reverend," or "Father," was a shock in itself. (This was actually the first Protestant church I'd ever set foot in as an adult. Talk about leading a sheltered life!) But Mo was right about the teaching. It was wonderful. I felt I got more out of just one of Terrys Scriptural messages than all the sermons I'd ever heard in the Catholic Church put together!

Without fully realizing it, however, we were starting to embrace biblical truths that crossed doctrinal red lines, so far as the Catholic Church was concerned.

Our acceptance of being born again, for example, was at odds with the church's traditional teaching of what made you a Christian. The position of the Church, as I mentioned earlier, was that you became a child of God when you were baptized as an infant. This practice is Scripturally incorrect on two counts. Obviously, an infant is incapable of

PENANCE

understanding the gospel and making a decision to accept Christ, so water baptism clearly should not take place until after the child has reached the age of reason. And even more importantly, not until after he or she has been born again. We see that order demonstrated in the conversion of the apostle Paul in the ninth chapter of the Book of Acts. And also in the story of Cornelius in the tenth chapter.

Apparently, the understanding about first being born-again fell off the radar screen many centuries ago and was replaced with an empty religious ritual, namely infant baptism. Just as the experience of the baptism of the Spirit was replaced by the laying on of hands in the sacrament of confirmation.

At best, infant baptism is a nice family ceremony expressing hope that someday this little one will accept Christ as Savior and become a child of God. At worst it is a form of the longstanding pagan belief of baptismal regeneration, which gives one a false assurance of salvation. It took the upheaval of the Reformation and the blood of countless martyred saints to restore the foundational truth that a spiritual rebirth, not a water baptism, is required to make you a child of God. Rome, of course, continues to view this teaching as heretical.

However, it wasn't long before we started bumping into other church practices we once had accepted without question. Like the Sacrament of Penance. Why should we have to confess to a priest and do penance for our sins, we wondered, if Jesus has already done all the penance needed by dying on the cross? We had seen in Scripture that all our sins had already been forgiven. And if we sinned again, all we had to do was confess them directly to God, *"...and He is faithful and just and will forgive us our sins and purify us from all unrighteousness"* (1 John 1:9).

In 1 Timothy 4:3, we read that it was a doctrine of demons to forbid marriage or advocate abstaining from certain foods. Yet all Catholic clergy are forbidden to marry. And for years we had been told not to eat meat on Friday.

In Matthew 23:9, it says not to consider any man on earth our spiritual father, *"for you have one Father, and He is in heaven."* Yet every priest expects to be called Father.

And what about the centrality of Mary in the Church? We couldn't find anywhere in Scripture support for her assumption into heaven, her immaculate conception, or her perpetual virginity (she clearly is reported to have naturally mothered four more boys and at least two girls besides Jesus in Matthew 13:55 and Mark 6:3). Nor is there any mention of her being a co-redeemer. Or co-mediator with Jesus (refuted by 1 Timothy 2:5). Or being the Mother of God. Or the Queen of Heaven. All one finds is the story of a young Jewish virgin girl being chosen by God to miraculously become the mother of Jesus. Blessed among women, most certainly, but nothing more.

I remember when we shared some of our findings about Mary at a Thanksgiving gathering at Mo's parent's house. A sudden tension came into the room. Most of the family was cutting us a lot of slack, but my mother-in-law drew the line at Mary. After she came to the Lord and escaped Catholicism herself she told us that we had come within an inch of getting hit with a ladle full of mashed potatoes that night.

One day we came upon this Scripture: *"And every priest stands daily ministering and offering time after time the same sacrifices, which can never take away sins; but He having offered one sacrifice for sins for all time, sat down at the right hand of God"* (Heb. 10:11,12, NAS). Not only was penance unnecessary now, but obviously there was no further need for sacrifice either, whether Jewish or Christian.

What then was the Holy Sacrifice of the Mass all about? For we had been carefully taught that in the Mass we are participating in a bloodless sacrifice of Jesus whose body and blood were present on the altar in the form of bread and wine. And that this sacrifice was "efficacious" towards sin, sanctification, and the assurance of salvation.

In spite of our growing list of troubling questions, Mo and I continued to attend Sunday mass faithfully. In that respect, we were like a child who moves the vegetables he doesn't like to the corner of the plate and keeps on eating. We just assumed that with a little spiritual renewal these incongruities could be straightened out and the Church would be back on track and everything would be fine again. We still did not see any real conflict with what we now believed and remaining Roman Catholic.

But it doesn't take a meteorologist to figure out a big storm was coming!

Chapter 5

The Bridge Church

Having seen firsthand the transforming power of the baptism of the Holy Spirit and were convinced it was just what our parish needed to gain new life. So we decided to introduce the Charismatic Movement to Father Sal. The best approach, we felt, was to ask him to invite a charismatic priest to speak at the church, perhaps at a communion breakfast. We'd met several friendly priests at the Bridgeport parish when taking the Life in the Spirit seminar, and a couple of them had already told us they'd come and speak.

We felt pretty confident Father Sal would be receptive to our request because he'd recently allowed us to start a folk mass on Saturday nights. This lively guitar-strumming type of mass was being steadily introduced into Catholic churches around the country, but had not come to our parish yet. So taking the initiative, we gathered a few young girls we knew who could play guitars, and a few parishioners who loved to sing, and asked Father Sal if we could liven up the liturgy on Saturday night. Surprisingly, he agreed. Soon attendance at that mass soared. Surely, we figured, he would be open to this suggestion as well.

The plan was to invite Father Sal to a casual Sunday-night dinner at our home and make our request there. Our hopes soared when he accepted our invitation.

On the night of the dinner, Mo prepared a delicious beef stroganoff, one of her specialties. In spite of a heavy rain, Father Sal showed up right on time and the three of us sat down to dinner. We'd gotten the kids to bed early so we

Valley of the Steeples

could talk without any interruption. During the meal, we kept the conversation light and friendly, not wanting to talk about "business" quite yet. After the plates were cleared, and he was relaxed, sipping an after-dinner drink, I casually brought up the subject of having a visiting priest speak about the Charismatic Movement.

It was like somebody threw cold water in his face. Instantly his friendly demeanor disappeared. "Ab-so-lutely not," he hissed, emphasizing each syllable to make his point. Then leaning forward he fixed me with the coldest smile I'd ever seen, and added, "And what are you going to do about it?" Stunned by his unexpected hostility, I responded that we'd probably have to go someplace else. Until that moment that was the furthest thing from my thinking, but he'd left me no choice. With that awful smirk still firmly in place, he replied simply, "Remember, you said that...not me." Then, without another word he got up from the table and walked out of the room. I heard him collect his rain gear out in the foyer, open the front door, and leave.

A heavy stillness descended upon the house. In that moment, I knew that man was not my pastor. For the Holy Spirit immediately quickened to me a verse from the Gospel of John that I had read recently. *"The Good Shepherd lays down his life for the sheep. He who is a hireling, and not a shepherd, who is not the owner of the sheep, beholds the wolf coming, and leaves the sheep, and flees ... He flees because he is a hireling, and not concerned about the sheep"* (John 10:11-13 NAS). It was the beginning of the realization that <u>Jesus is our one and only Pastor.</u>

As we cleaned up, Mo and I could almost feel the shackles falling off. A divine euphoria suddenly swept over us. We sensed some great spiritual battle had just been fought in the heavenlies on our behalf, and we had been handed the victory. We knew we'd been set free from something!

The next day, we took our kids out of the church school and put them in public school. And when Sunday came, because we now were churchless, we just stayed home. Having never missed church so deliberately before in our lives, we felt like two kids playing hooky. But we didn't feel the least bit guilty about it. Somehow we knew we had God's permission to just stay home and worship Him in our hearts. So we just sat out on our deck and read our Bibles with the kids that morning, truly enjoying the peace and quiet of a Sunday as never before. God's presence seemed to hover in the air, while the birds sang sweet praises to Him in the treetops.

At the same time we knew it was only temporary. You can't stay out of church forever, can you? We figured we'd check out the neighboring Catholic parishes next week and join one of them. But God soon redirected our thinking.

One evening that week, as I was reading in the Book of Revelation, I came to the 18th chapter which contained a description of the Great Harlot, the City of Babylon. I was immediately struck by its remarkable likeness to the Vatican which I'd visited a few years before when we were filming a TV commercial in Rome. Babylon's trappings were described as... *"fine linen and purple and silk and scarlet, every kind of citron wood and every article of ivory...costly wood and bronze...incense and perfume and frankincense and oil...."(Rev. 18:12,13).* All these things I'd seen in my visit to St. Peter's.

I called out to Mo, who was in another room, to come and listen to this. Starting again from the first verse again, I began to read aloud. When I came to the fourth verse, the words cut through the air and penetrated our hearts: *"Come out of her my people that you may not participate in her sins and partake of her plagues."* I stopped reading and looked up at Mo. Both of us knew instantly we had just heard the voice of the Lord. And that we were being told not to go back into the Roman Church—ever again.

We immediately bowed our heads and prayed, "Lord, where then should we go to church?" Suddenly, St. Paul's, the charismatic Episcopal Church where we'd been attending Bible studies, came to mind. The more we considered St. Paul's, the more we believed that was exactly where the Lord was directing us. It would be the first time in memory that any member of our family had left the Catholic Church.

The following week we paid a visit to St. Paul's. Even though we had been going there for the Monday-morning and Wednesday-evening Bible studies, we had not yet attended a Sunday service. The Sunday service, to our mind, was the official service for true members. So to make sure we did everything correctly we set up a meeting with the assistant pastor, a personable young man named Renee Scott, to join up officially. Again the title of "Reverend" and "Father" was dismissed.

The first startling thing we learned was that we couldn't join St. Paul's because they didn't have a membership list. If you came, you came. If you didn't, that's okay, too. They were just there to minister to whoever God sent.

If that wasn't shocking enough, we then learned they didn't use donation envelopes or require financial pledges. In the Catholic Church we'd always gotten a year's supply of "gift" envelopes in advance which we were expected to fill with money and deposit in the collection basket each Sunday. But this young priest told us that at St. Paul's they didn't burden the congregants with envelopes and pledges— they just trusted God to provide. And He always did. Clearly,

St. Paul's was a very unconventional church. In fact, it was not unusual to see visiting bus loads of church groups show up to see what God was doing there. (You can read the story of this amazing church in, <u>Miracle in Darien</u>, by Bob Slosser.)

I'll never forget that first Sunday morning that the Hennessy family showed up at St. Paul's. Walking down the aisle, I felt we had "Roman Catholic" emblazoned across our foreheads. Of course, it didn't help that we genuflected before entering the pew as all Catholics do, and all Episcopalian don't. Worse, we brought all four of our kids with us into the church, including ten-month old Todd, again not realizing Protestant kids don't sit in the service but go to Sunday school classes or into a nursery. But nobody had told us that. Part way through the service I panicked when I realized there weren't any other kids around. I thought, "Good grief! Catholics are the only ones with kids. Everyone else must all be using birth control!" Mo and I laughed later when she told me she had the exact same thought. We felt like spiritual rubes. But when you've just come out of the Tenth Century, spiritually speaking, it takes time to adjust to reality.

The service itself was surprisingly similar to the Roman Catholic rite, which helped us relax a bit. The officiating priest, who again was Terry Fullam, was dressed in long vestment robes like the Catholic clergy. The liturgy also had about the same number of opportunities to stand, sit and kneel. And the service lasted about the length of a Mass. Of course, we knew that Episcopalians had a different interpretation on communion than the Catholic belief of transubstantiation. That is they taught Christ was only present in the wine and bread spiritually—not physically, as we were taught to believe. <u>When you think about it, how could the bread and wine at the Last Supper be the physical</u>

body and blood of Jesus? He was sitting right there with them in the only body he had. And He certainly didn't hack off a piece of Himself and give that to His apostles.

As communion time approached, I noticed they weren't passing it out the same way as in a Catholic church. Back then, Catholics knelt, stuck out their tongue and the priest would place the wafer in your mouth. But here they were handing it to the people and even giving them a sip of the wine, which we never got. Not wanting to make any mistakes up there, I turned to the woman next to me and quietly asked her to explain how it worked.

Smiling sheepishly, she said: "I'm not sure. I'm a Catholic."

"Really?" I replied.

Undaunted, I tapped the man in front of me on the shoulder and asked the same question.

Turning around, he lifted up his hands in a helpless gesture, and said, "Sorry, it's my first time here. I'm a Lutheran."

This was getting interesting. Turning to a woman behind me I tried again. Another Catholic.

Looking over at Mo, I whispered, "Aren't there any Episcopalians here?" Obviously, this church was attracting folks from all over.

The best part of the service, of course, was the teaching of Terry. He just opened up the Bible in a way that left you feeling completely nourished spiritually. In addition to his teaching skills, he was also a wonderful worship leader. So at the worship time he came down from the altar to sit at a small piano to lead the whole congregation in song. As he did, the place just exploded to the rafters in loud, joyful singing. It was so different from the listless, mechanical singing we were used to as Catholics.

At the end of the service, nobody wanted to leave. Everyone just stood around talking to each other and sharing stories and hugging and laughing. This too was unlike what went on in a Catholic church, where the parking lot would be empty minutes after the last words of benediction were spoken.

Several people came over and welcomed us and told us how God had brought them there. It seemed everybody in this church had an amazing story of being led there from some other church by the grace of God. Eventually, we did meet some of the original Episcopalians who were thrilled at what God was doing in their church.

For us, coming to St. Paul's was like coming home. We finally felt we were among people who knew and loved God as much as we did. Everyone there genuinely cared about you. Not just the clergy, but the people, also. In describing the place to others, we'd say, "when you walked through the doors of St Paul's, love just smacked you in the face!"

Sitting under the teaching of Terry Fullam every week, caused our spirits to blossom and grow strong. Like dry branches, we soaked up every drop of living water pouring forth from the anointed ministry in that church. We often say that everything we ever learned about being a true follower of Christ we learned there. Or at least was reinforced there, because the Holy Spirit is truly the only One who can teach us anything. Teachers can teach, and preachers can preach, but if the Holy Spirit doesn't say something to our heart, we won't hear a thing.

One thing I heard loud and clear was Terry say that he could think of no greater tragedy in a person's life than to die without ever knowing why he was born. Right then and there I committed myself to discovering and carrying out God's highest purpose for my life. Eternity was a long time to spend thinking about how or why I missed it.

Later, as God began to reveal more about the true fellowship of believers and worship under the New Covenant, I wondered greatly about St. Paul's. If the organized church was as much of an obstacle to the gospel as we finally saw it to be, how and why was St. Pauls such a blessing? It was so spiritually invigorating there, that every church we visited afterwards, paled by comparison.

I believe there are several explanations.

First, freedom was paramount at St. Paul's. As Mo likes to say, "unlike most churches, they always left the back door open." The goal of leadership there was to help us grow strong in the Lord so we could follow Him. Not them. And if the Lord was leading you on, then you were simply graduating. When you combine that freedom with the servanthood, teaching and the great anointing of love that abounded in that place, how could you not be spiritually invigorated?

Second, there was Terry Fullam himself. Uniquely gifted in music, leadership and in the ability to teach the Bible, he had been sovereignly called by God to this church. While leading a tour in the Sinai Desert, God spoke to him and told him that when he got home he would receive an invitation to pastor a church (something he never wanted to do), and he was to accept it. It was St. Paul's who gave Terry that call. Yet in spite of his many gifts, he was a very humble man who was always reminding the congregation that he was not the head of the church—Jesus was. And that we, the congregation, were all priests.

I recently found an old teaching tape of his, where he even corroborated the message of Mo's vision. Listen to his words: "God does not dwell in St. Paul's, people. He never has. He dwells only in you. When you come in, He comes in. And when you leave, He leaves. It's as simple as that."

Third, I believe God had a specific purpose for raising up a St Paul's and Terry Fullam at that time. Although Christians from many denominations, and even a few Jews, were being awakened by God through the charismatic renewal, they needed solid Biblical teaching to grow. Especially those who came from the more rigid sacramental churches like Catholics, Episcopalians, and Lutherans who would never get that kind of teaching in their home churches. (God made sure Terry's influence wasn't limited to Darien, Connecticut by having his teaching tapes sent all over the world.)

We realized later how blessed we were to have experienced St Paul's when we encountered a number of charismatic Catholics who didn't get that teaching and were unable to shake free of the errors of Catholic dogma. They eventually became even more imprisoned in their allegiance to their Church as time went on.

The Episcopal Church, I have since learned, is called the "bridge church." So when God brought Terry to St Paul's, I believe He was providing a bridge out of sacramental Christianity for all those trapped behind enemy lines, so to speak. To accomplish this, God had to give this former Baptist teacher the highly unusual desire of becoming an Episcopalian priest. Once inside the system, he could now deliver the kind of pastoral teaching that no Catholic, Lutheran or Episcopalian had heard in centuries. But he could do no more. He could lay a foundation of truth for the Holy Spirit to build on, but he was not called to expose the root of the malignancy, the system itself. How could he and still function within the system? But this often caused his teaching to conflict with the very platform he preached from.

For example, he correctly preached that all believers are priests of God (as 1 Peter 2:9 declares). Nevertheless, at St. Paul's only members of the clergy wore priestly robes and were allowed to serve at the altar. Visually, his priestly attire and clergy privileges were cancelling out his own words. *"Thus you nullify the word of God by your traditions that you have handed down"* (Mark 7:13).

The same when Terry correctly taught that Jesus did not dwell in the building of St. Paul's. Again, the vaulted ceiling, altar and attending priesthood overwhelmed the message. More than words would be needed to drive home the transforming truth of that message and separate us from the delusion the building wasn't truly God's home. Especially since many of those sitting in the pews had been trained from childhood to remove their hat, lower their voice and even bow their head when entering a church sanctuary in reverence to the presence of God.

Again, when he correctly taught that Christianity was not a religion, the trappings of religion everywhere fought against that truth. As the saying goes, the medium is the message. Only the power of the Holy Spirit in that place allowed the life in his words to overcome the religious traditions.

But 1976 wasn't the time for focusing on the lie of religion. It was the time to get a lot of newly awakened baby believers, like us, up and running.

As you might expect, we immediately began to talk up St Paul's to all those friends and relatives who had followed us through marriage encounter and the baptism of the Holy

Spirit. Pretty soon car loads of folks were following us to St Pauls and then coming back to our house afterwards for more fellowship. Both during the week and on Sundays. As we added these busy activities to our marriage encounter meetings and other responsibilities, we soon found ourselves distracted from our primary responsibility—our kids.

It all came to a head one evening at one of our encounter gatherings. I forget the actual details, but one of the couples had really begun to annoy us. Instead of being honest about our feelings (and their behavior), we had kept silent. In the course of the evening something was said and it triggered in me an outburst of anger. They immediately responded in kind. Although we all quickly calmed down and asked each other for forgiveness, the evening left us very unsettled. It felt like a satanic attack—and it had come through me.

When we got home, we told my mother who had been babysitting the kids, what had happened. She then went home and we went to bed. The next morning the phone rang. It was my mother calling to say that the Lord had awakened her during the night and given her a message for us. He'd said, *"Tell Maureen and Brian I love them. Jesus lives in their home. The children are first."* The message had an immediate comforting effect on us following last night's ugly experience. But it was also an unmistakable wake-up call to get our priorities straight concerning our children. As a result, we dropped out of the marriage encounter meetings and started spending more time focusing on the children. As Mo often says today, we can easily trip over our ministry on our way to our ministry.

Now that we found St Paul's, Mo and I thought we could finally just relax and enjoy our new church home for years to come. But God had other plans. He was about to send another holy upheaval into our lives. This time it would happen at my place of employment.

Chapter 6

Madison Avenue and God

My day had started routinely enough. I'd taken the 7:55 train from Stamford to Grand Central Station and I was now walking the two and a half bone-chilling blocks up 43rd street to my office.

As I hurried along, I noticed a few people with black smudges on their foreheads and realized with a start it must be Ash Wednesday. A sense of relief washed over me knowing I would never again have to join them in that arcane ritual that just outed you as a Roman Catholic. And I gave thanks to God once again for all the amazing things He was doing in my life.

Before heading up to my office, I turned into the little snack shop just past our building for a roll and coffee, as I did every morning. Entering the warm, crowded shop, I was surprised to see my boss, Jack Dalton, coming towards me clutching his white coffee bag. I'd never seen him in here at this time before because of our different train schedules. As I was about to wave him a "good morning" in passing, he stopped in front of me. "Glad I bumped into you, Brian. When you finish your coffee, come by my office. I'd like to talk to you about something." I said I would and proceeded to get on line as he left, wondering what this was all about.

The company where I worked was not only one of the largest ad agencies in Manhattan, but it had been in the forefront of a revolution of creativity in the industry since the late fifties. Although a number of hot new shops had since joined the revolution, like the one where I got my first job, this was still the mother ship and the place you wanted to work if you were a creative person

I had been employed there as a copywriter for almost ten years, and Jack had been my copy group head for nine of those years. He was the senior writer on one of the agency's biggest accounts and I was his number two writer. But he also had supervisory responsibility over two other accounts where I was the primary writer. I enjoyed working for Jack. He was a fair man and an excellent ad writer. At 51 he was 16 years my senior and was sort of father figure to me in my rapidly advancing career. He was also an ex-Navy commander who ran a tight ship.

After quickly polishing off my roll and coffee, I walked down the hall to see Jack. I just figured a new assignment had come in with special instructions that he wanted to fill me in on. I had no clue the next few minutes would change the course of my life forever.

"You wanted to see me about something, Jack?" I asked, knocking and entering his office at the same time. He motioned for me to take a seat as he got up from his desk and went over and shut the door. I knew that wasn't a good sign—unless it was going to be about a raise. But that didn't seem likely since I'd just received one a few months before. Taking his seat again he got right to the point.

"Brian, there are two topics that traditionally shouldn't be discussed in the work place: religion and politics. I'm telling you this because I've been told by top management that someone complained about you bothering them with religious talk. You need to cease and desist from doing any more of it."

Now it was true I had been speaking to several co-workers about God as a result of the spiritual awakening in my life. In fact, just a few days earlier I had briefly shared some of the amazing events of my God story with Jack himself. So there was no use denying it. But I hadn't exactly been cornering people in the conference room to talk to them about Him. Nor was I interrupting anybody while they were working. In fact, almost all my conversations began as a result of someone coming into my office with some personal tale of woe. After listening politely for a few minutes, I'd tell them I wasn't a marriage counselor or a psychiatrist or whatever professional service equated with their problem. But I did know someone who could solve any problem—namely Jesus. And I'd go on to tell them more about Him and my recent experiences with God. I quickly related all that to Jack and told him I was sorry if I offended anyone, I certainly didn't mean to.

"It's not important who starts the conversation," Jack replied. "You just have to knock off the religious talk, period." Leaning forward he continued, "I want to make myself perfectly clear, Brian. I've been told that if you don't stop, your job could be directly affected."

Having delivered this message, he paused and then looked me straight in the eye and asked, "So, do I have your word that you will stop talking about God or Jesus around the office?" I felt my heart sink down into my socks.

How could I say yes to such a request? But how could I say no? A spirit of fear swept over me as I realized I was cornered and had to make a decision. But in that moment a miracle took place. A verse from the Bible suddenly floated up into my consciousness and filled me with strength and courage and the certainty of what I must do. The verse, as I discovered later, was in the Book of Acts. It told the story of Peter and John when they had been summoned before the chief priests and the elders and told not to speak or teach in the name of Jesus. Their answer was: *"Whether it is right in the sight of God to give heed to you rather than God, you be the judge; for we cannot stop speaking what we have seen and heard"* (Acts 4: 19,20).

    I didn't hear all those words. I just caught the sense of the whole scripture in my spirit. In the next moment I heard myself saying, "I'm sorry, Jack, but I can't make that promise. If one person came to know Jesus through something I said, that would be more important to me than even my job."

    I guess he thought he hadn't heard me correctly because he asked, "Would you say that again?" So I repeated it. Heck, I couldn't believe I'd said it myself. Jack just stared at me then not saying anything for what seemed like a month. I suddenly felt sorry for him. I realized he was now the one in the very difficult position.

    Finally I broke the silence and said, "I'm sorry to put you in this situation, Jack. But that has to be my final answer." Not knowing what else to do, I stood up and walked out of his office.

    That night I told Mo all that transpired at the office. Her immediate reaction was that it sounded very scriptural, so there was nothing to worry about. "Wasn't that just what Jesus said would happen?" she reminded me. "Didn't He tell us not to bother preparing a defense in advance when they haul you into court? That the Holy Spirit would tell us what to say?"

    Although we didn't know what would happen because of all this, we both sensed God was again doing something major in our lives.

    Over the next few days, nothing changed much in my work routine. It was almost like the whole conversation in

Jack's office never took place. I had thought the powers-that-be would hit me with some kind of penalty for my refusal to toe the line, as Jack had indicated, but when nothing further happened I assumed they just forgot about it. But they hadn't.

Their response was to slowly start withdrawing my work assignments. It happened so subtly that I didn't even make the connection until months afterwards. As my present work load wound down, I suddenly found myself without any new assignments. I'd go into Jack and tell him my availability and he'd just say we were slow right now. But if anything came in he'd let me know.

Pretty soon I was in a full work drought. I'd spend the whole day with absolutely nothing to do but thumb through industry magazines and stare out the window. I soon started bringing my Bible to work just to pass the time. I'd close the door to my office and spend the whole day reading this Book that I had ignored for the first 35 years of my life. I had to laugh. Only God could arrange the circumstances that would allow me to read my Bible everyday—and get paid for it. But the thrill wore off pretty quickly and was replaced by a growing agony over my frustrating situation. I felt trapped between two worlds. My heart and soul were focused on knowing more about God and the Bible, but my life and finances was tied to a career that was now torturing me.

The weeks dragged on until Easter was almost here. Mo and I had been praying every night for a solution to my dilemma. But every day was just more of the same boredom. Worse, in spite of my bold declaration to Jack about talking to my co-workers about God, I noticed I wasn't. If I did have an opportunity to say something to someone, I would quickly glance around to see who was listening. The joy I once had

Valley of the Steeples

in sharing my spiritual insights was gone. Fear had taken its place.

Leaving the office after one particularly difficult day, I decided I'd had enough. I would just quit my job and go work in a hardware store, or a bookstore. Anywhere but where I was.

Relieved at having made this decision, I settled into my seat on the train. As the train pulled slowly out of the station I opened a Christian book I'd been reading, Lord of the Valleys, and turned to the place I'd left off. The next chapter heading was entitled, Don't Jump the Fence. The chapter went on to warn that when God has you hemmed in for a time in a difficult pasture, don't try to get out by jumping the fence. Wait on Him to open the gate. If you try to escape too soon you'll just have to repeat the experience somewhere else. But if you wait for Him to open the gate in His perfect timing you will be able to move on and do so with God's blessings.

I realized with a start God was actually speaking to me through this author. He was telling me He understood the difficulty of my situation, but I was to hang in there a little longer, that a time was definitely coming when he would open the door for me to leave. I immediately scrapped my dumb idea about working in a hardware store, which wouldn't have solved anything anyway, and with new resolve committed myself to waiting for God to deliver me. (It was during this time that Mo had the vision of the valley with the church steeples and Jesus crying.)

It didn't take long for God to keep His promise. About two or three weeks after Easter the gate suddenly sprung open and I was free.

It happened like this.

After dinner one night I picked up a Christian newspaper that had come in the mail, and with Mo looking over my shoulder, I started to thumb through the pages. In doing so, I was struck by the number of large ads promoting Bible colleges on almost every page. Suddenly, it was like God was shouting at me, "Go to Bible college, Go to Bible college!' Maureen heard it, too. In that moment we both somehow knew my advertising career was over and we were going to Bible college, even if we didn't know where yet. We were so excited we could hardly get to sleep that night. (I always tell people, when your wife can get excited about you quitting your job, you know it's God.)

That weekend we picked out a couple of colleges from the paper that looked interesting and ran them by our pastor, Terry Fullam, for his opinion. He told us we probably wouldn't feel too comfortable with any of our choices because they weren't charismatic. He suggested instead a new, interdenominational charismatic college in Anaheim, California, with the unlikely name of Melodyland. Since we had just read a book about a minister from that school we took it as a confirmation from God and applied for admittance for the fall semester. The next step was to go in and give my two-week notice at work.

Jack didn't seem at all surprised when I told him I was retiring early, which is how I put it to him. (At this point I still hadn't connected the dots as to why my work had dried up.) He told me he would miss me, but that he understood. He later took me out to a farewell lunch and told me that he had encountered this type of "religious phenomena" before and typically the individual's work declined soon afterward. But he had to admit that the jobs I completed were some of the best work he'd ever seen me do. I just thanked the Lord for giving me a good witness to this man who had been watching me so closely.

My last two weeks at the ad agency were thoroughly enjoyable. Free of the cloud of fear that had hung over me, and still with no work to do, I was able to roam about the agency to say goodbye and tell everyone why I was leaving. That opened up wonderful conversations with a number of co-workers about God, who had no idea all this was going on in my life. Years later I bumped into one of the men, an art director, who told me I had so influenced him with my sharing that he had started a serious search for God himself and had found Him and been born again. Thank you, Jesus!

The supreme irony came when I, who had been ordered to shut up about Jesus around the office, found myself in the heart of the agency, the creative director's office, witnessing to him and several others about the love of God for over an hour. God sure has a sense of humor.

On Friday, May 14, 1976, which was also our tenth wedding anniversary, I said good-bye to my exciting thirteen-year career in advertising and took the commuter train home for the last time. Now I had to get ready to sell our home and move my family of six to California. It hit me later that I had quit my job <u>before</u> I had received my acceptance from Melodyland. Mo and I had been so full of faith adrenaline that we had just plowed ahead without ever thinking I might <u>not</u> be accepted. Wouldn't we have looked silly if I had been turned down? Thankfully, my acceptance letter came a few days later and the "for sale" sign went up on the front lawn of our wonderful home.

As the preparation for our departure proceeded, the enormity of what we were doing crashed in on me one day and I had to sit down and catch my breath. Did I really just walk away from an exciting, high-paying career that had been so fulfilling? And am I really selling this beautiful home that had we had worked so hard to obtain? All this so we could head out into an unknown future? I had always looked at my life as kind of a board game. If you advanced your piece according to the rules, and applied time and patience and good work, you would eventually achieve success. Now I had taken my piece off the board. How could I ever win now? Was I nuts? Did I have a nervous breakdown—as at least one family member had already suggested?

"Oh, Lord," I prayed, "I trust You completely. You said You would never leave me or forsake me. You said You would show me the way to go. Please reassure me and confirm again I'm doing the right thing here."

As I shifted my attention back on Him and off myself and my scary situation, a peace descended and my joy and excitement quickly returned, and soon I was back packing and cleaning out. In the months and years ahead this, "Oh, Lord, are You sure?" kind of prayer would become a regular staple in my life as God would lead us further and further out on the limb of trusting Him, and Him alone.

Although at first we intended to fly to California, we later decided to make the trip a more leisurely, fun-filled vacation for the kids in order to minimize the culture shock. To accomplish that we bought a 20-foot, Dodge motor home that was named "Little Champ." It was big enough to sleep us all, but still small enough to drive comfortably in traffic and on the highway. Our plan was to take the northern route, Interstate 90, across the country and see every site of interest we could along the way. Our furniture would go ahead on a moving truck and we'd just retrieve it when we arrived. If we left on August 12th, we figured we'd arrive just in time for school enrollment.

We still didn't know if we'd rent or buy a home out there. But there was no doubt we'd be moving into smaller quarters. That meant we had to get rid of a lot of stuff. Some we gave to family. Some we sold to friends who promised to pay us later. Some we gave to charity. And the rest we unloaded in a garage sale at greatly reduced prices. By mid-July, all that remained to be sold was the house itself. But even though it was getting close to departure time, we weren't worried. We were catching on to God's *modus operandi* for building faith, which was don't expect anything to happen until the very last minute. Later we'd learn that God was free to change even His own methods, especially when we start to expect Him to act in a certain way.

It was about a week before we were to leave that finally a man who had looked at the house a month earlier came back and purchased it. I remember the puzzled look on the man's face as he said, "Why am I doing this? I really don't want this house." But he signed the agreement, anyway. He didn't understand he had just been recruited to play a part in God's divine plan. He must have grown to love the house later, just as we did, because I know he stayed there for many years afterwards.

Since the house sale came so close to our moving, we had to give our lawyer power of attorney to close in our absence. That money, which would net us about $60,000, was what we planned to live on for the next three years.

The Lord then did two things that allowed us both to leave with greater peace of mind. First, my mother finally decided that she disagreed with more teachings in her Catholic religion than she agreed with. Therefore, in order to be true to herself she could no longer remain a Catholic. She sent a letter to the entire family announcing that she was leaving the Church, listing every doctrine she now found to be untrue and giving the Scriptures that refuted them. She then joined St Pauls, where we knew she'd be fed spiritually and be among folks who really loved her.

The other good news was my father was delivered from alcoholism and was on the road to recovery. Faced with impending retirement, he had started to drink more and more, which led to a whole mess of dysfunctional activity. But we had gained new hope for him when we read a couple of books by Merlin Carothers, a retired army chaplain, about the power of praise. This author taught that praise was the answer to every situation. His teaching, which acknowledged the complete sovereignty of God in all things, was based on Romans 8:28: *"God causes all things to work together for good to those who love God, to those who are called according to His purpose" (NAS)*. He recommended not only praising God out loud in whatever unhappy situation we were facing, but also for the problem itself. Not that we had to like the problem, but rather to see it simply as the stuff God was using to bless us and deliver us and accomplish His purposes. Using the life of Joseph, he showed how God used his brother's hatred to get him to Egypt so he could rescue them all later from the drought.

He shared how he himself was initially skeptical about this principle and asked the Lord how he could praise Him and thank Him for a horrible problem? The Lord told him, "Look at my son on the cross. Would you have praised Me for that horrible death at the time?" Carothers got the point.

His first book, Prison to Praise, was so successful he wrote another one sharing all the stirring testimonies of people who had taken his advice and gotten wonderful results. The first testimony in this book was about a young married couple who had an alcoholic dad who was set free soon after they started praising God for his condition. The story was so similar to our situation, we felt it was the Lord showing us this was the answer. So Mo and I immediately got on our knees and thanked God that he was in charge of my father's life, and for using even this drinking for my father's good. We released him to the Lord, praising Him and thanking Him. Immediately we felt the problem lift from our shoulders and with it came the assurance He'd take care of it. To make a long story short, my father was completely delivered from drink within two weeks. Although he did have a relapse years later, we saw firsthand the power of praise. And the best news of all was that shortly before he died in 1986 he received Jesus as his Lord and Savior!

The last Sunday before we left for California, we attended service at St. Pauls one last time. It was a sad moment for us, knowing we'd be leaving these wonderful people, and this wonderful place that had nurtured us into spiritual personhood. But God made certain we didn't leave without a proper sendoff. Entering the church we bumped into Renee Scott, the young assistant pastor. He was obviously the one conducting the service that day since he was wearing the official Episcopal priest getup. I chuckled to myself as I recalled how he himself often would joke about these robes, saying, "You call me father, but I stand up here dressed like your mother."

Greeting us with a big smile, he suddenly remembered that we were going to Bible college and asked when we were leaving.

"Wednesday," I told him.

"In that case, how about if I call you and Mo up around communion time and we'll pray for you?"

I said that would be great and thanked him.

At the appropriate time in the service he made good on his promise and we came forward and knelt at the altar rail.

He then laid his hands on our heads and asked the whole congregation to call on Almighty God to lead us, provide for us, and bless us in this step of faith we were taking. By the time he was finished praying, tears were streaming down both our faces. I realized the Lord had just given us this moment as an emotional closure to our time at St. Paul's.

We were ready to move on to the next stage of our spiritual journey. From then on we referred to ourselves as graduates of St Paul's, Class of '76.

The home we left behind in Stamford, Conn.

A family photo, 1976.

Chapter 7

California Dreamin'

The day for us to hit the road finally came. Friends and family gathered in our driveway to see us off, including my mother, who was probably taking our departure the hardest. After a round of hugs and tears and promises to keep in touch, and with all of us waving goodbye out the camper windows, I steered the Little Champ out of our driveway, not knowing if we'd ever be back this way again. I doubt Christopher Columbus felt any greater sense of wonder at what lay ahead of him than we did.

Before traveling too far out into the wilderness, we decided to stop and visit Mo's younger sister, Kathy, and her husband, Jerry, at their home in Quakertown, Pennsylvania. They lived in a wonderful, old Pennsylvania Dutch stone farmhouse on 70 acres of farmland with their two-year-old son, Brad. Like so many others in the family, Kathy and Jerry had listened to our testimony as it evolved, believed it, and made Jesus Lord of their lives. Kathy, however, was still having a hard time letting go of the Catholic Church. But Jerry had no such problem. He owned a restaurant and was always working on Sunday anyway, so he was glad to be rid of the guilt for always missing Mass.

We wound up staying five days on the farm, mainly because a rare hurricane, Hurricane Belle, washed across the northeast for several days and kept us from venturing back out on the highway. But we didn't mind. It allowed us to spend more time with Kathy and Jerry and Brad, since we knew we probably wouldn't see each other for awhile. As it turned out, that time together was a divine preparation for a return visit that would last a bit longer.

It took us three weeks to cross the country in our RV, stopping at KOA campgrounds all along the way. I won't take time to describe our exciting, fun trip across the United States, except to say that the Lord is a wonderful travel agent. Every day seemed pre-planned. There'd be some unique natural or man-made attraction for us to explore each day with the kids; a scenic view to cause us to appreciate the beauty of America; and always a KOA to pull into and park our RV at the end of the day. Some days we'd only drive 50 miles, other days 500. And as Mo's diary reveals, gas prices ranged between 58 cents and 65 cents a gallon back then. The good 'ole days! But the best times for Mo and I were, driving down the highway after supper, sipping a cup of coffee, and watching the sun set quietly behind some mile-long corn field or purple mountain peak. That's when the amazement at what God was doing in our lives would impact us the most. We'd just keep saying to each other, "Can you believe where we are?" Then we'd just praise the Lord, knowing He had a KOA somewhere up ahead we would soon call home.

By the time we reached Anaheim, however, we were all ready for larger living quarters. The excitement of living in a motor home wears off quickly after three weeks. We found a motel for the night, which seemed like a palace by comparison, and the next day I got busy tracking down more permanent housing.

The only lead I had was the name and number of a woman real estate agent the school had given me as a possible housing contact. I called that number and got the realtor's answering service. Although the person told me the woman was on vacation and had left strict instructions not to forward any calls, nevertheless, she immediately dialed her number for me. Thank you Lord!

The realtor, who was as surprised as I was that I had gotten through to her, gave me the only rental lead she had. It was a four-bedroom rancher five minutes from the school. Although presently occupied by several Melodyland students, she believed they were moving out.

We drove over to the house and found one of the students home. He showed us the place and confirmed they were indeed leaving in a few days. They had finished school in June but unlike most graduates they had decided to stay the summer to take some extra classes. We realized later that God had used them to preserve the house for us.

But before we agreed to take the house, we decided to investigate other options we might have. So we drove around looking at houses for three days, hemming and hawing about what we should do. Should we buy a home? No, too expensive. What about other rental possibilities? We couldn't find any. So, finally, we returned to the student's house, signed the lease, and told the movers where to deliver our furniture. Since we couldn't move in for a couple days, we knew just what to do. We headed straight for Disneyland with the kids and rode everything in the Park. Although we'd come here in pursuit of God's Kingdom, we would spend a lot of time in the Magic Kingdom, as well.

After we moved into the house we discovered how big a miracle this house was. We learned all the rentals in the area had waiting lists, if you could find one. Furthermore, our house had four bedrooms and a bumped-out dining room which was unusual for this style home. Of course, if the Lord is your realtor, all things are possible! The Lord even had to fend off other interested parties for three days as we casually drove around trying to make up our mind. Another student told me later he tried to get the house during that time but could never catch up with any of the students who lived there.

Our next step was to check out the school, which was literally right across the street from Disneyland. Melodyland, as we discovered, was both a church and a school. The concrete church building, which was designed in the shape of a large round, ochre-colored tent, was once a theatre for broadways musicals. Hence, the name. When it didn't succeed, Ralph Wilkerson, Melodyland's pastor, purchased the building and created one of the country's first mega churches. Later he added the interdenominational, charismatic Bible college, which I soon discovered to my surprise was actually a seminary for the training of pastors. It had never occurred to us that the three-year Master of Divinities program we'd signed up for was a pastoral program. We just wanted to study the Bible, and the Holy Spirit had led us here. Since I felt no desire to become a church pastor, nor Mo a pastor's wife, our first thought was we'd missed God's leading somehow. But the Lord quickly calmed us down and assured us we were definitely where He wanted us. And this was certainly confirmed by subsequent events.

At first opportunity, we attended a service in our new church home. Compared to the warm intimacy we enjoyed at St. Paul's, and the lofty formalism we'd grown up with in Roman Catholicism, this church was a mind-blower. With over three thousand people seated in a round, amphitheater-like setting, the service opened with a number of lofty hymns performed by a full orchestra and choir before the pastor ever stepped onto the raised, circular blue-carpeted platform in the middle of the arena. It was Christianity gone Hollywood, where big-name Christian entertainers often made guest-speaker appearances. The baby-sitting and children's Sunday-school classes alone rivaled the logistics of a full-scale military campaign. And all this was repeated three times every Sunday morning with a healing or deliverance service usually scheduled in the evening.

Overseeing this Christian wonderland was a full staff of pastors and assistants, mostly from Pentecostal backgrounds. It was definitely a big-time operation. At first it dazzled us and made us feel we were on the cutting edge of things. Later it all grew a bit thin.

Our real church home turned out to be a small group of students and their wives the school had put us together with that met weekly in one of our homes. Most in the group were about our age, married, and had left careers in order to attend Melodyland. Only one young man, in his mid-twenties, was still single. These folks became our true fellowship and our core social group. We also befriended several neighbors, including a Christian family across the street that we stayed in contact with even after school. Next door lived a retired couple who had recently gotten saved and delivered from Catholicism. You can bet we had a lot to talk to them about.

We quickly enrolled Tara, Chris and Brendan in the local public schools, which were just starting. Since we had enough money from the sale of our house, Mo didn't need to work so she stayed home with Todd while I attended classes. We purchased a new Dodge Volare station wagon for Mo (only $5000 in 1976!) so she'd have some wheels, and I took the Little Champ to school. I soon found it was a good place to study and do homework between classes.

In the middle of the first semester, Mo and I felt a push from the Holy Spirit to get re-baptized. The church had a large baptismal tank and periodically held baptisms for all those willing to take this step of obedience. Since we now considered our infant baptisms as meaningless, we felt it was time to do it right. When we told our children what we were doing, our oldest, Chris and Tara, said they wanted to be baptized also. We explained to them that water baptism was like the Israelites going into the Red Sea and coming up on the other side, free from the clutches of Pharaoh. It signified that we had died with Christ and been resurrected with Him, thereby delivering us out of the kingdom of darkness into God's kingdom. The next day we all took the plunge as a family. God even used the occasion to finally release my prayer language. When I came up out of the water I burst into tongues, praising God!

For the first year, everything proceeded pretty normally. We quickly settled into California living, which isn't hard to do when the sun is shining every day and the temperature is always around 80 degrees. As Californians like to say, "Oh well, just another boring day in paradise."

While I poured myself into my studies and hands-on ministry training, Mo typed my papers, encouraged me, and kept the household running smoothly. Going back to school at thirty six was a bit weird at first, but I quickly got back into it and began getting the best grades of my academic life. It's amazing what a little maturity and knowing the Lord can do for your schoolwork. The subjects offered covered the Old Testament, New Testament, Greek, Hebrew, church history, systematic theology and other church or Bible-related topics. They let you pick and choose what courses you wanted to take, as long as you completed all the required ones by graduation.

I discovered that the Holy Spirit was definitely the best instructor on campus. In my Old Testament class, for example, the instructor had assigned two large, expensive textbooks written by liberal German theologians. Right from the start there was grumbling in the class from a few students who had come out of liberal Protestant churches and didn't want to hear any more from those kinds of scholars. The grumbling broke out into open rebellion in the classroom about three weeks later. The teacher who was truly trusting the Spirit and being obedient to His leading concerning the assigning of those books, immediately fell to his knees in front of the whole class and cried out to God. "Lord, I know you specifically led me to assign those books. Help me now. I don't understand and cannot explain why!"

Instantly the Holy Spirit fell on the class. I can't speak for what the others heard, but the voice of the Spirit resonated loudly within me, *"I am the way, the TRUTH, and the life!"* With the emphasis on the word '*truth.*' Instantly I understood He was telling us that if we have Him we don't need to store up knowledge. The Lord was confronting the false notion that we were there to learn a bunch of theological arguments to go out and do battle. He wanted us to know He is like the Library of Congress. We just have to trust Him for all the answers, not rely on a lot of head knowledge.

This experience taught me never to judge another man's walk or work for the Lord. What doesn't make sense to us could still be God's leading in his life. It was a lesson I would shortly be taught again—but this time as the one with the questionable leading.

It was at the start of my second year that God began to show me the main reason He had sent us to Melodyland. It was to answer the big question that had been gnawing at the back of my mind, namely, how did the church get so far off track? In the Book of Acts we see the early Jewish believers going forth with the message of salvation and turning the Jewish world upside down. Then, after Paul receives the revelation that Gentiles can be included in the promises to

Abraham, the church explodes worldwide. So what caused it all to go so wrong and end up as the Roman Catholic Church? How could so many believers have wandered so far astray for so long? Who fell asleep at the wheel?

The answer to that overall question began innocently enough when I took a class on church history taught by an Episcopal priest. As an interdenominational school, the teachers as well as the students hailed from all across the Christian spectrum. It was really an ongoing experiment in Christian togetherness.

On the first day of this class, this priest casually referred to the legitimacy of the apostolic succession of bishops in the middle of making a point. My ears shot up. That was a central doctrine of the Roman Catholic Church I was very familiar with. It taught that a bishop could trace his authority back through a line of bishops to the Apostle Peter. It was based on the false notion that Jesus had left behind a human successor, namely Peter, to run things in His absence. And that He had then given him authority to choose a successor. Of course, such a concept completely ignores—and usurps—the role of the Holy Spirit.

I wondered how such an unbiblical doctrine as that could be promoted here at Melodyland? I thought this was the great charismatic response to all such institutional theology that wanted to stifle the authority of the Holy Spirit.

After class, I approached the teacher and voiced my concern. I suggested that according to the Book of Acts, that if any man could be said to be in charge of the church after the ascension of Jesus it probably would have been James, the Lord's physical brother. Or perhaps the apostle Paul. But even if it was Peter, there were no Scriptures to support that Jesus gave him any authority to delegate a successor. He seemed stunned that I would even question this doctrine, and had no ready answer.

A bit stunned myself, I immediately switched out of his class. In its place, I selected a class called, The History of Christian Thought. It sounded a bit dry, but it was the only choice left at this late date. This class, taught by a young man about my age who was a Presbyterian, focused on the writings of the so-called Apostolic Fathers and other great Christian thinkers who lived during the first five centuries. He warned us that their writings, compared to the loftiness of Scripture, would "feel like we were falling off a log." They were that uninspiring.

Nevertheless, it soon became obvious he held these writers and their works in high esteem for, as he put it, "the contribution they made to the evolution of Christian theology." However, as we began studying these revered men I was shocked to see embedded in their writings all the seeds that grew up to become the doctrines of the Catholic Church. The more I read, the more I realized it was their teachings that had spawned the institutional church system.

Clement of Rome, for example, promoted the doctrine of apostolic succession (the doctrine I challenged the previous professor on) that eventually led to the hierarchical system and the division of clergy and laity.

Ignatius of Antioch's teachings were heavily influenced by the mystery religions, especially Mithraism, which taught that a believer could become divine by eating the flesh and blood of its deity in a sacramental meal. It isn't hard to see how the Catholic priesthood and doctrine of transubstantiation could evolve from that.

Justin Martyr relied on Platonic philosophy to explain the death and resurrection of Jesus and opened the floodgates for relying on pagan thought to interpret Scripture. For example, Cardinal Henry Newman, an 18th century English intellectual who had converted to Roman Catholicism late in life, argued in his autobiography, Apologia Pro Vita Sua, that "pagan literature, philosophy, and mythology, properly understood, were but a preparation for the gospel" (pg. 632, English Prose of the Victorian Era, Oxford University Press). In other words, Newman saw the pagan writers as early prophets, a divine provision for the gentiles who had no access to the revelation given the Jews. In effect, this put their "wisdom" on a par with Scripture. And he readily credited the church fathers for giving him this understanding.

Others like Origen, Cyprian, Tertullian, Clement of Alexandria, even the great Augustine, all ignorantly contributed doctrinal error in their attempt to interpret the teachings of Christianity through pagan lenses. Even my hero, St. Thomas Aquinas, basically employed the philosophy of Aristotle in all his theology. That's not to say that all the writings of the church fathers were corruptive. It seems many of their homilies were very inspiring.

As the semester progressed, the Holy Spirit began to put it all together for me. I saw that as the centuries advanced church leadership began to look back more and more to the words of the church fathers for guidance. Increasingly, their writings were accorded a certain mystique because they wrote so close to the events that took place in the first century, putting their words almost on a par with Scripture. Councils were called and doctrines and creeds were formulated based on positions they had taken in their writings. And, slowly but surely, the church moved off the bedrock of inspired scriptural truths onto the shifting, sinking sand of man's reason. We were taken *"captive through philosophy and empty deception, according to the tradition of men, according to the elementary principles of this world, rather than according to Christ"* (Col. 2:8 NAS).

This was possible because a major cultural shift took place at the end of the first century. The nation of Israel was sent into exile, the city of Jerusalem destroyed, and all the original Jewish disciples of Jesus passed from the scene. As a result, church leadership and the proclamation of the gospel were now under new management. And it was all Gentile.

Unlike the early Jewish leaders who had grown up with the Scriptures, which Christians call the Old Testament, and who with the help of the Holy Spirit could interpret the many types and shadows and prophecies as they related to Jesus, the new Gentile leaders had no such background to draw from. Converted from various forms of paganism, they were steeped instead in Greek philosophy, mythology, mystery religion, and the powerful framework of Roman organization that prevailed across the Empire.

In their zeal to defend and define the new faith, and to steer us away from Jewish hopes and promises for which they had little sympathy or understanding, they began to intermingle ideas from other sources. Soon the entire message of grace and salvation by faith became obscured by their theologies. And in its place a gospel of works righteousness arose with religious roots that stretched backed to pagan antiquity. Thank God we still have the original inspired writings of the Jewish disciples, which we call the New Testament, together with the prophecies and promises of the First Testament in the Bible. Otherwise we would all still be making pilgrimages to Rome and getting burned at the stake for any doctrinal deviations.

By the Fourth century, the writings of these Gentile scribes had laid the theological foundations for a powerful new religion that came to be known throughout the world as Christianity. When Constantine arrived on the scene in early 300 AD, a Christian religious theology was now in place. He just recognized Christianity as a legitimate religion, promoted it to the chief religion of Rome for his own political purposes, and as Emperor appointed himself chief priest over it with the title of Pontifex Maximus (Supreme Pontiff). This title was later assumed by the Bishop of Rome and shortened to "Pope."

Church buildings, which hadn't existed for the first three hundred years of the church's existence, soon came into existence. Many had been former pagan shrines that were simply converted to Christian use. Pagan holy days had their names changed and became Christian holy days. Even the names of pagan gods were later altered to become the names of Christian saints. And just as those divinities were associated with different professions and given a daily feast day, Catholic "saints" were accorded the same honor. All this was done to appeal to the pagan world to make it easier for them to join this new religion.

Of course, it can't be stressed enough that faith in Jesus is not a religion in the traditional sense. The word "religion" comes from the Latin word, "religio," which means "the binding upon a people." Although any set of beliefs that address our origins and ultimate destination can be considered a religion, such as atheistic humanism and Buddhism which have no deity, traditional religion usually includes a deity, a priesthood, a shrine, and a sacrifice of some kind. In that sense, we do not have a religion.

As Sir Robert Anderson points out in his book, that prior to Constantine, "the State required that all Roman subjects should profess some religion, but the Christians, who had neither altars nor priests, neither sacrifices nor images, were held to have no religion at all... so they were looked upon as atheists, and punished accordingly; and even by such enlightened rulers as Trajan and Marcus Aurelius" (Types in Hebrews, pg. 153).

So now I knew how the church was derailed. These men were truly the fathers of the religious hierarchical institution that is represented from the majestic dome of St Peter's in Rome to the quaintest country chapel in rural Arkansas.

The very day I received this divine download from God, the Lord sent someone to confirm it so I wouldn't think I was imagining things. In the following class, a dear brother from our home fellowship, Fred Stevens, leaned over and whispered, "As I was just praying, I saw your face in a vision, and I saw scales falling from your eyes." Since I had not said a word to him about my understanding of the church fathers, I knew God was letting me know what I had just seen was true.

However, as obvious as this truth now was to me, not everyone else could—or wanted to—see it. I figured, surely the teacher in the class knows all this to be true. But when I approached him about it, even telling him about my perspective from a Catholic background, he disagreed. He recognized the errors in their teaching, but he was unwilling to take these men down from their historic pedestals and label their writings poisonous. He thought their contributions outweighed all their negatives. That opened my eyes even wider and made me wonder if the charismatic movement wasn't already going back to sleep?

Brian and kids and
the Little Champ in Nevada desert.

Mo and the kids at Disneyland, CA.

Chapter 8

The Calling

Another major development that semester was the arrival of Mo's younger brother, Joe, and his girlfriend, Sue. We had stopped in to visit them for a couple of days in Arvada, Colorado when we drove home to Connecticut for summer recess. Joe was pursuing a career in music as the lead singer in a band. That path had led him to Florida where he met Sue. Both decided to hook up and head west. Colorado was as far as they got.

Prior to our arrival at their Arvada apartment Joe had warned Sue not to bring up the subject of God because he'd heard we'd turned into "Jesus freaks." Which was true, I guess. But he didn't realize that Sue had a growing hunger in her heart to know God. So she couldn't wait to meet us.

Well, we all had such a wonderful time together, that after we left, they decided to move to California and get closer to us and to Hollywood where Joe felt his music talent might be more quickly discovered. So while we were in Connecticut, they moved into our home in Anaheim until they found their own place in a nearby town.

But God had more in mind for Joe and Sue than having him make it big in the music business. In fact, soon after they arrived their fortunes took a nose dive. Neither could find a good paying job and they quickly found themselves getting more and more depressed as their funds and hopes dwindled. Naturally we began encouraging them to trust the Lord. We sensed God was just using their deteriorating circumstances to get them to a point of total surrender so He could reveal Himself to them in His perfect timing. Especially Joe, who was not exactly looking for spiritual answers in his life just then. Every time another job prospect would go sour for Joe, Mo would sing, "Give it all, give it all to J-e-s-u-s!" And he'd just laugh at our silly beliefs and go out try again.

This went on for weeks. Then listening to a Christian radio station one day we learned about a man who was carrying a large wooden cross around the world, named Arthur Blessit. The announcer said he was going to be at Hollywood and Vine at noon that day. Our curiosity peaked, so we took all the kids and Joe and Sue and drove into Los Angeles to see this strange sight.

Sure enough, there he was walking along the street toting a huge cross that had a roller skate wheel on the back end for mobility. A small crowd was gathering around him as he loudly preached about Jesus Christ. This was a rough area of the city, as we quickly discovered, similar to what Times Square was also in those days. Prostitutes, junkies, homeless people, winos—you name it, were all standing around on the sidewalk and in doorways. Just the kind of people Jesus wanted to help most. Drawn by the sheer showmanship of Arthur's bizarre cross and the power of the Holy Spirit, many started to follow after him—so we just joined the parade. Pretty soon we all came to a vacant ball field where Arthur invited everyone who wanted to meet Jesus to assemble in front of him and he'd pray for them. When Mo and I looked, there was Joe and Sue up there with their heads bowed praying along with Arthur Blessit and everyone else. That day we gained a new brother and sister in the Lord!

As Joe and Sue began to learn more about their new spiritual life, Sue made a surprise discovery. She was pregnant. Later, when Joe was reading his Bible while sitting in a wooden shack working as a night watchman, he heard the audible voice of God say to him, *"I've just given you a son."* When he came home he told Sue what God had said and they both rejoiced.

This good news quickly precipitated their desire to get married, and a couple of weeks later we had a wonderful, Holy Spirit orchestrated wedding celebration in our back yard. One of the pastors from Melodyland conducted the ceremony, and a family up the street, who had a wedding the day before, contributed all the flowers and chairs. And Mr. and Mrs. Joe Torpey joined our little extended family. Thank you, Jesus!

Between my mind being blown about the church fathers and all that was going on with Joe and Sue, it was becoming a wild semester. But it was another class and another revelation from the Lord that would initiate another new chapter in our life.

In this other class we were studying the physical characteristics of ancient Israel as described in the Bible: the topography, architecture, flora, fauna, foods, customs, etc. The idea was that greater understanding of the details in the biblical stories would yield greater insight into the larger message of the stories. The only requirement for passing this course was to write a paper on one of those physical characteristics. I chose to write on leaven.

I had been fascinated by leaven ever since I noticed the important role this seemingly innocuous substance played in the religious life of Israel. Prior to the night of the great exodus from Egypt it had played no role at all. But on the night of the tenth plague, God suddenly instructs Israel through Moses to memorialize that night by annually observing the Feast of Passover and another feast: the Feast of Unleavened Bread. To celebrate this feast the Hebrews were instructed to remove all leaven (*seor*) and leavened bread (*chametz*) from their houses for seven days (see Ex. 12:15). The reason both substances were banned, I discovered, was because both were contagious and capable of infecting a third substance. So serious was this command, that to disobey would result in being cut off from the community.

It was the severity of the penalty, banishment from the nation, that caught my attention. What was it about leaven that would cause God to employ such wrath? There must be a reason. I decided a term paper was just the place to do my investigation.

God had even prepared me in advance that summer by arranging for me to meet a Jewish baker who told me about his special leaven. It seems this leaven, or yeast as it is more commonly called, had been in his family for decades. His father had carefully brought it to this country from Europe after the Second World War. He claimed this leaven gave his bread "the zing his competitors could only dream about." He even showed it to me. It was a grayish lump that he kept in a pan. It smelled awful. He told me it was alive and that he had to feed it unsold bread scraps at the end of the day. I felt I was looking at death.

I learned that leaven is actually a micro-organism that causes a bio-chemical reaction to take place in the dough called fermentation. This corruption of the dough releases carbon dioxide, causing it to rise and become "leavened." Unleavened bread, on the other hand, remains flat as a cracker, like a Saltine, which the Jews call matzah.

It didn't take me long to see that leaven was freighted with a lot of spiritual principles.

I realized first, that symbolically, leaven throughout the Bible is always a bad thing. Leaven itself (*seor*) represents the ancient lies of Satan that we swallow as they come to us imbedded in the wisdom of the world's teachings (*chametz*). We see this confirmed when Jesus tells His disciples to beware of the leaven of the Pharisees and Sadducees. It took them a few minutes to get His meaning, but they finally realized, *"he was not telling them to guard against the yeast used in bread, but against the teaching of the Pharisees and Sadducees"* (Matt 16:12). These false teachers were the very ones Jesus had accused of being sons of the devil, the father of lies. Through their half-truths these teachers were disseminating Satan's lies through their positions of influence and corrupting the spiritual life of His people, Israel.

False teachings, once accepted, evolve into traditions that lead God's people astray and cause untold suffering and death for generations. *"Thus you nullify the word of God by your tradition that you have handed down"* (Mark 7:13).

I realized that God was using this term paper to show me once again how the evil influence of the church fathers had corrupted the whole life of the Body of Christ. But even more exciting, I saw God's solution to the leaven problem revealed in the instructions concerning the Feast of Unleavened Bread. According to the divine mandate, the leaven must be completely removed. Under the Old Covenant it was the home that had to be thoroughly cleansed of the physical substance of leaven or leavened bread. But under the New Covenant it is our thinking and practices that must be purged of anything that contradicts the revealed truth of God as confirmed in the Bible. Wherever we encounter any of the world's corrupting wisdom in our belief system, we are to discard it. We cannot allow even the smallest trace to remain, because, *"A little leaven leavens the whole lump of dough"* (Gal. 5:9 NAS). It's like a dandelion. If you don't get the whole root, it will just grow back.

Therefore, once a teaching or tradition is discerned as false, no matter how venerable it might be, it must be abandoned. If we allow it to remain as any part of our thinking it will eventually rise up and corrupt our behavior all over again. Years later I realized this was the reason the Protestant Reformation failed to deliver us from the influence of Rome and the evil fruit of the church fathers. It tried to *reform* the Catholic system, rather than perform radical surgery. Although the Reformers jettisoned much of the false doctrine and practices of Rome, they continued to cling to the organizational concepts of Roman Catholicism.

As one church history author noted, "Even though the leaders of the Protestant Reformation sincerely intended to break with the traditional Roman Catholic conception of the church, nevertheless, the tradition arising from the Reformation did not succeed in making the break" (Hendrick Hart, *Will All the Kings Men*, Wedge Publishing Foundation, p 30).

The Reformers simply modified and adopted the unscriptural Roman Catholic concept of organized church life for their own purposes and settled down again. From an organizational standpoint, it truly was just a re-formation of the same old thing. Which is why we are still dealing with the death sown through the ignorance of the church fathers today?

In the process of writing the paper I also discovered the telltale sign that lets you know when leaven (error) is present in a particular teaching. It was pride. Any teaching that is based on reasoning rather than revealed truth will soon cause a person to become pride-filled. *"Knowledge puffs up, but charity (love) edifieth"* (1Cor. 8:1, KJV). That is, love builds up, but knowledge gained from worldly reasoning puffs up a person—or a church—and ferments strife and other works of the flesh. That is why a church group will usually stop loving you and start persecuting you when you disagree with their theology.

I realized the word "theology" itself is just a pompous term used to describe man's carnal reasoning about God and His teachings. It is a Greek word that means "the study of God." Can you imagine anything more arrogant than the creature putting the Creator under a microscope to study Him like a bug? And then putting our flawed deductions on the same level as the Word of God in a creed or church doctrine?

And here I was at a school of theology!

The day I turned in my term paper, I told Mo that I think we'll be leaving school sooner than we expected. However, before I would leave school, God had one more thing to tell me. Something far more personal.

He chose a time between classes when I was alone in my camper reading my Bible. I had recently committed myself to reading through the entire Bible and I was now up to the 18th chapter in the Book of Deuteronomy. When I came to the 14th verse, where Moses is instructing Israel about entering the Promised Land, I read, *"For those nations, which you shall dispossess, listen to those who practice witchcraft and to diviners, but as for you, the Lord your God has not allowed you to do so."*

As I read the last words of that phrase I felt them being addressed to me personally: *"...but as for you, the Lord your God has not allowed you to do so."* It gave me the sense of being singled out by God for a special assignment. I immediately stopped reading and looked up from the page. I hadn't forgotten what God had said to me about being born for a unique purpose on that first marriage encounter weekend. It caused me to ask out loud, "Lord, who am I?"

Looking down at my Bible again, my eyes fell on the next verse where Moses suddenly announces the coming of a future prophet to succeed him: *"The Lord your God will raise up for you a prophet like me from among you, from your countrymen, you shall listen to him"* (Deut 18:15 NAS). I sat stunned as I realized God was using these words to answer my question. He was telling me I was that prophet. Time seemed to stand still for me in the camper. I could barely breathe. I finally whispered, "Lord, how can this be?" No angel appeared to confirm the words I had just heard in my spirit. No voice from heaven trumpeted forth any further assurance. I tried to grasp what I'd just read and could not take it in. It was incomprehensible. Yet I knew I had just heard from God, so somehow it must be true. As I slowly yielded to the overwhelming reality of the calling God was placing upon my life, I began to cry.

The day was November 20th, 1977. I know, because I wrote the date in my Bible right next to the verse.

It is now thirty years later as I type these words, almost to the day. And I still cannot fully comprehend the enormity of what God said to me. How many times have I considered the audacity of even thinking such a thing? Just sharing them now is a huge step of faith for me. Who am I, indeed! It is like being told you will hit a game-winning grand slam home run in the ninth inning of the last game of the World Series, when you never played more than sandlot baseball and are too old now to even swing a bat. There is no way to rationalize it. Yet over the years I have allowed myself to wonder when... and how? And to ponder just what or where or who "Egypt" is today? But as often as I considered these questions, I said nothing about it to anyone for years. Not even Mo.

A week later, God did confirm that what He told me in secret truly was from Him. Again He used my good friend, Fred Stevens. As I was getting out of Fred's car after a late evening Hebrew class, he said to me in his quiet way, "Brian, I have a word from the Lord for you. It's Exodus 3:12."

I immediately opened my Bible and read the verse. It was God's commission to Moses to go to Egypt and set His people free. *"And He said (to him), 'Certainly I will be with you, and this shall be the sign to you that it is I who have sent you; when you have brought the people out of Egypt, you shall worship God at this mountain."*

I was speechless. I wanted to ask Fred a thousand questions, starting with, "Did God tell you what this really means as it relates to me?" And, "Did he tell you anything *more?"* —but I couldn't open my mouth. I was too filled with false pride or false humility, whatever that is that makes you feel embarrassed about being chosen for a special task, to even tell Fred this confirmed what God had just told me eight days earlier. So I just thanked him, shut the car door, and went in the house. I told Mo what Fred had said, but said nothing to her either about it confirming the Deuteronomy promise.

The next day, in the privacy of the camper, I reread the Scripture Fred had given me like a secret love letter. Then I noticed the words Moses uttered when God told him of his mission: *"Who am I, that I should go to Pharaoh...?"* (Ex 3:11) It was the very same expression I had blurted out, although he seemed to be asking it with a lot more humility.

Over the years I searched for all the references I could find about this Moses prophecy. I found seven. Deuteronomy 18:15 is the only place it is clearly mentioned in the Old Testament. The other six references are found in the New Testament. In the Gospel of John it is mentioned four times. Twice the Baptist is queried by the people if he is the Prophet? Or the Messiah? Or Elijah? (John 1:21,25). Which implies the Jews saw them as three different personalities. John denied he was any of them. And on two occasions Jesus is thought to be either the Prophet or the Messiah (6:14, 7:40). Again the perception is they are two different people.

The last two references are found in the Book of Acts. In Acts 3:22, 23, the exact words of Moses about this coming prophet are repeated by the apostle Peter. But before he quotes them, he declares that Jesus, who had gone up into heaven, would not return *"until the restoration of all things about which God spoke by the mouth of the holy prophets from ancient time"* (Acts 3:21 NAS). Peter then follows this observation with the Moses prophecy, inferring the Prophet will be a catalyst in God's hand for inaugurating that long awaited and often prophesied restoration.

The final reference is in Acts 7:37, when the disciple Steven is on trial for his life. In the midst of his discourse he too mentions the Moses prophecy.

All these Scriptures tell me the Prophet could not have come before or during the first century. That his appearance was still future. I realize that virtually all teaching on the subject today assumes the Prophet's role was fulfilled by Jesus. But it was not. The Prophet is not the Messiah. He is not deity. He is just a man, as Moses was. In fact, God tells Moses that very thing. *"I will raise up a prophet like you."* He is just one more human servant of the Lord born of human parents called to accomplish a certain task in the anointing of God. Of course it is Jesus to the degree that it is He who is accomplishing everything through us, no matter what the work of our ministry.

One aspect of the Moses prophecy that baffled me for awhile was the stipulation that this Prophet would come forth from "your countrymen." That he would be an Israelite. I'm not Jewish, so how could the Lord ever apply this prophecy to me, however it will be manifested? But one day the Lord showed me that all believers are included in the chosen line of Abraham through faith in Jesus. *"If you belong to Christ, then you are Abraham's offspring, heirs according to promise"* (Gal 3:29 NAS). I realized my inclusion into this chosen family was real and actual, not just some spiritual badge of honor. And if you have faith to accept it, I believe all followers of Jesus are almost certainly lost physical descendants of Abraham scattered among the Gentiles. Father God would know who we were and where we went and could lead each and every lost, chosen descendant to faith in Jesus, Israel's Messiah, at the right time. Remember Jesus said, *"No one can come to Me, unless the Father who sent Me draws him"* (John 6:44). And, *"I was sent only to the lost sheep of the house of Israel"* (John 15:24).

I hope to write another book soon explaining how our true identity is really found in Abraham, not in a gentile religion. That is, our faith in Jesus not only makes us sons of God but brings us into the physical family of Abraham as true Israelites, not into Christianity to become "Christians".

With all these marvelous revelations I'd received, I knew our time at Melodyland was over. At first, we thought we'd just stick it out to the end of the school year in June so the kids wouldn't have to switch schools mid-year. But then we realized we'd exhausted almost all our money. That convinced us to head home in December. But where was home? We knew Stamford, Connecticut was too pricey for us to go back there. After praying about it, we both agreed the only place we could go now was Pennsylvania, where Mo's sister lived.

When Joe and Sue learned we were leaving, they said, "well, we have no reason to stay. We're leaving, too." So we all started making plans to go back east. All my classmates were shocked that I was leaving before getting my degree, but when I explained we had heard clearly from the Lord, they relaxed and accepted our decision.

A few days later, as I was packing, I started thinking about all my friends at Melodyland completing school and being ordained for ministry and I suddenly felt a little empty. Like I hadn't finished what I'd started. And if I felt that way, I could only imagine what some of my relatives and friends back home would think. But later in the day the Lord spoke to me through Leviticus 8:33: *"And you shall not go outside the doorway of the tent of meeting for seven days, until the day that the period of your ordination is fulfilled; for He will ordain you through seven days" (NAS)*. I heard, in effect, *"don't worry about getting a degree or man's ordination, I will ordain you when the time is right, and not before."* And I was fine with it after that.

Once again we called the movers to take our furniture, while we planned to drive cross country in the camper, this time with the Volare in tow. A neighbor, Paul, who was a Christian Volkswagen mechanic, disconnected the drive shaft in the car for us so it could be towed. His wife, Myrna, a Jewish believer, also gave us a plaque with a Scripture she had hand-lettered that hangs in our hall to this day. It reads, *"I will instruct thee and teach thee in the way which thou shalt go. I will guide thee with mine eye"* Psalm 32:8. It was a promise from the Lord that enabled us to walk on water in the months and years ahead.

In mid-December, 1977, we said goodbye to sunny California and headed back east, taking the warmer, southernmost route along Route 10. If we pushed, we could arrive at the Meyer's farm in time for Christmas.

Chapter 9

Down On the Farm

As we headed east on our fourth cross-country trip in two years, the Lord used the time to give us a quick post-graduate course in walking by faith. It would become valuable preparation for what lay ahead, although we didn't realize it at the time.

With the December temperatures starting to drop, we decided to skip the KOA campgrounds and stay in motels. But since this route served up long stretches of barren terrain between towns, that demanded a little more travel planning. So each morning we'd turn to the Lord and ask Him to provide a nice, reasonably-priced place for the six of us to sleep and eat at day's end. And off we'd go down the highway playing our Christian praise and worship songs.

Sure enough, just as it got close to dinner that first night in New Mexico, we drove into a small town with a nice motel. When I went in, the desk clerk told me they were all out of regular rooms, but he had a honeymoon suite that he let us have for the same rate. Praise the Lord!

When the Lord wonderfully provided for us again the second day, I felt Him clearly saying to us, *"If you will completely trust Me, I will always give you the best. Not the most luxurious necessarily, but My provision will always be perfect for your needs. But you must trust me 100%."* The flip side of the message, of course, was that I wasn't to revert to relying on my own ability to try and figure things out.

The following day turned out to be a pop quiz to see if I'd learned the lesson. I flunked miserably.

We'd been driving through barren Texas flatlands all day and we were tired and hungry when we pulled into the next town around six o'clock. We could only see one motel so I parked and went inside. Right away I didn't get a good feeling about the place, or sense the peace that told me this was God's best provision for the night. But I knew the next town was two hours away with probably nothing in between but sagebrush. So rather than trust God to provide something better, I took matters into my own hand and booked a room. It was a disaster. We were all crammed into two queen-sized beds and kept awake half the night by party revelers in the courtyard, cursing and smashing beer bottles. We started getting concerned even for the safety of the Little Champ when we heard them start mocking the Christian bumper stickers on the camper.

Arising at dawn, we couldn't move fast enough to put that motel in our rearview mirror. But as we drove off down the highway I looked to the right and noticed a lovely little motel just on the outskirts of the town. I didn't hear the Lord say anything, like *"this is where you could have slept last night peacefully if you had trusted me for the best?"* He didn't have to.

Two days later we started seeing Pennsylvania corn fields outside our windows, some still with patches of snow in the furrows from an early season storm. It was the first snow we'd seen in 3000 miles, and soon we were all singing along at the top of our lungs with Christian singer, Evie Tornquist, *"Come on ring those bells, light the Christmas tree, Jesus is the one, born for you and me!"*

We arrived at the Meyers farm in Quakertown late in the day on Christmas Eve. Kathy and Jerry welcomed us once again into their small, but cozy three-bedroom, one-bath stone farmhouse. This time we'd be sleeping in the dining room since it was too cold to sleep in the camper as we did on our previous visit. Their family had grown since our last visit with the birth of their little girl, Becca, the previous year. With us, that brought the total number of people living in the house to ten. There wasn't a lot of gift exchange that year, but it was one of the merriest memories we have of Christmas as we all bundled together in that happy home with their big, warm fireplace.

Joe and Sue, who had arrived a week earlier, were living temporarily in a tiny, two-room cottage on the property of Jerry's restaurant. However, the apartment shared a thin, common back wall with a similar unit. The tenant behind them was a single woman who on the weekends liked to entertain long into night. Although appreciative for Jerry providing this 'port in a storm,' they still fondly refer to that place as "The Pit."

After registering the kids in school, our next priority was to find permanent housing. Knowing the truck with all our furniture was due to arrive in three weeks, Kathy quickly lined up some rentals for us to look at. But everything we saw was either too small, too rundown or too expensive. One or two times I almost said to Mo, "maybe we could make this work." But then I remembered that little motel in Texas on the outskirts of town and said, "no, I don't think this is it. I know God has something better for us."

Soon, only a few days remained before the truck was scheduled to arrive and we still had no place to put our furniture. We could probably store it in Jerry's barn if we had to, but then we'd have to move it again. But as it turned out, the Lord had everything under control. The next morning we got a surprise call from the moving company saying they were very sorry, but our truck had broken down in Chicago. They were bringing in a new truck and driver, but it would take another week or two before they switched loads and got to Pennsylvania. We told them it was not a problem and to take their time. And breathing a huge sigh of relief, praised the Lord who truly runs the entire universe.

In between house hunting trips with Kathy, I started seeking God for clear direction about what we were supposed to do here in Pennsylvania. One day, as I walked around Jerry's property praying, I suddenly heard the words in my spirit, *"Come out of the city and dwell in the field."*

"Lord," I replied, "how do I do that? It's winter! Do you want us to live in our camper? I'm willing, but…are you sure?"

The next morning while reading my Bible I came upon Micah 4:10. And there it was again: *"For now you will go out of the city, dwell in the field…"* It was obvious the Lord was giving me some important instructions. But what did it mean? Puzzled, I could only file it away for future clarification.

We'd been squeezed into Kathy's and Jerry's now for about a month and the pressure was growing to pick a house, any house. Then a blizzard hit and blanketed the whole area with over two feet of snow. That put our house hunting on hold for a few days until they got the roads cleared. It was so bad, Jerry even had to use a snowmobile to get to the restaurant.

Although we were stalled by the storm, Joe and Sue had made progress. They had been able to move out of "The Pit" and into a small, renovated farmhouse that they rented from Jerry's parents. It was too small for us, but perfect for them. Sue was now several months along in her pregnancy, and they needed a place to start building their nest.

Soon we were back out house hunting, but with no better results. Then, just when the situation was starting to look hopeless, Kathy heard about a Mennonite dairy farmer who had bought a farm just up the road in Coopersburg. It seems the farmer and his four sons had worked all summer fixing up the house but they didn't have time to outfit the barn before winter set in. Without the barn for the cows, they couldn't move in yet. Since Kathy knew the man she immediately called him and asked if he'd consider renting to her sister and her family. He told her to come on over and they'd talk about it.

The farmhouse sat way back at the end of a long gravel driveway, which meandered some 150 yards downhill across a creek bed and up the other side before stopping between the house and the barn. The vacant, two-story house had four bedrooms, a new kitchen, a new furnace, and new carpeting throughout. It had been freshly painted and was ready for someone to move in. It had "God's best" written all over it.

After talking to us and learning we were Christians, the farmer and his wife decided we were the answer to their dilemma and offered us a year lease, which we took. The rent would be $325, due on the first of every month.

So after nearly six weeks of searching, we finally had a home. In God's perfect timing, the delivery truck called that afternoon to say they were in Quakertown. Did we have an address where could they drop off the furniture? "As a matter of fact, we do," we replied.

But that wasn't the end of the miracle. When the truck arrived at the house and the driver saw the long, snow-packed, ice-coated driveway he would have to navigate, he told me he couldn't risk slipping off that narrow passage and getting stuck in the field. He said we'd have to unload the furniture out on the street and carry it to the house. I knew that would take hours of back-breaking labor, so I asked him if we spread cinders on the ice, would he reconsider? He said he might.

Jerry, my indomitable brother-in-law, who had just come from the dentist after having all four of his wisdom teeth extracted, told me he knew where he could get a pickup truck full of cinders. A half hour later he was back and the two of us began shoveling gravel off the back of the truck, covering the whole length of the driveway. But when the driver inspected our work, he felt it was still too risky to attempt it.

I decided the situation called for a bold step of faith. I told the man that if he would attempt it, Jesus would keep his big rig on the road all the way down that driveway and back again. If he felt the wheels slip even the tiniest bit at any time, he could quit and we'd do it his way. He didn't look convinced, but he accepted my challenge. Slowly, cautiously, he crept down the entire length of the driveway and all the way up to the house without a single slip. When he parked, he jumped out of the truck and exclaimed, "That Jesus of yours really did it!" He knew something miraculous had just occurred.

But then the driver sheepishly informed us he couldn't help us unload the truck because he had a bad back. But God knew what we would need, because the farmer suddenly showed up with his four strong sons to give us a hand. I think we had that truck unloaded in less than an hour. And not a second too soon. The truck had barely departed, when a second winter storm blew in and dumped another two feet of snow blocking all access in or out of the driveway. But we were in!

A few days later, as I gazed out the window at the hundred or so acres of snow-covered corn fields surrounding the house, I realized that we had indeed *"come out of the city to dwell in the field."* The Lord had simply given me that word in advance to confirm to us later that we were definitely in the right place.

With all the excitement of coming back to Pennsylvania and finding a house, we had forgotten about our other big problem—we were almost out of money. In fact, after paying the moving truck and the first month's rent, we found we had less than a hundred dollars left. And that was it. There was no savings and no income to draw from.

The next 12 months would quickly become a chapter out of the life of George Mueller, the English evangelist renown for trusting God for all the money and provisions needed to run his orphanage in Bristol. This extreme faith walk we were about to experience would actually turn out to be the whole reason we were here in Pennsylvania. It would become a flesh-searing, white-knuckle roller-coaster ride where we learned how to trust God *"to give us this day our daily bread."* Although we may have casually mumbled those words before whenever we prayed the "Our Father," we never would again. In this experience I would be constantly challenged to justify my actions, not just to others, but also to myself.

Here's what happened.

Since I didn't know what work God wanted me to do yet, I decided the best thing was to sit tight until I did know. Mo agreed. Besides, this was hardly the neighborhood for reactivating my high-powered Madison Avenue career. Which, to be truthful, I no longer had a heart for anyway following my escape from New York. So there we sat on our snow-covered farm until the next rent was almost due. But before we had time to push the panic button, a check arrived in the mail one day large enough to satisfy the rent. It was

Valley of the Steeples

our security deposit from the home we'd rented in California. I'd written a couple of letters requesting it, but had gotten no response. I'd pretty much written off ever seeing it again. But here it was, just in the nick of time.

Besides the timely way that first check showed up, other money suddenly started arriving to meet our day-to-day needs. Mo started keeping a careful record of all we received. For example:

"March 28th - twenty dollars from Mom Hennessy.

April 6th - thirty dollars in the mail from an unknown caring person.

April 16th - ten dollars from Laura in church.

April 18th - fifty-eight dollars from Kathy and Jerry.

April 24th - twenty dollars from Joe and Sue. "

Whatever our need—milk, groceries, electric, phone, heating oil, gas for the car, whatever—the Lord miraculously provided just as we needed it. All of this greatly encouraged us to believe God was doing something very sovereign here and to get with the program.

However, the next month got a little more exciting. This time the Lord let us sweat a bit more, as it got to within one week of the rent being due without us having the money. When it got down to four days I went into a meltdown. Grabbing the Yellow Pages I quickly located one small in-house ad agency in the area and called them. When they didn't answer, I jumped in the car to track them down. After spending two hours and several gallons of precious gas driving up and down Allentown Road in a futile search, I returned home exhausted and depressed.

As Mo and I sat in the living room preparing ourselves for an eviction notice, Mo suddenly had an idea. "Do you think this would be a good time to call the Hunters and ask for the money they owe us?" David and Jill Hunter lived in Connecticut and were Christian friends who had bought some of our furniture in Stamford on credit with the promise to pay us when they could. So far they hadn't been able to.

In reaction to Mo's question, my first thought was to say "no." I remembered George Mueller had never asked anyone or told anyone he had a need. He let God tell them. But that was George, and this was us. "You know," I answered, "I think this would be an excellent time to give them a call."

As I got up and started across the room to make the call, suddenly the phone rang. Answering it, I could hardly believe my ears. It was David Hunter! And he was telling me he was in Quakertown, and asking where we lived? He wanted to stop by and see us. And then he said, "oh yeah, do you need some bread?"

"Sure do," I replied, thinking he was speaking about the money he owed us. I gave him directions to the house, and he said he'd be right over.

Mo and I started dancing around the room, praising God. We knew this was our miracle in the making. When David arrived he told us this long story about how a customer he'd done work for in New York asked him if he'd install a security alarm system in his home in Quakertown. Since David had heard we'd moved here, he said yes. He had just come from reviewing the job and wanted to see us before heading back to Connecticut. He then asked me if I would assist him with the installation and he'd pay me. I said sure. That was the "bread" he was referring to. We chatted for awhile, telling him about how we got here, and how we were waiting for direction from God, and after about an hour, with David not saying anything about paying us for the furniture and us not asking, he left.

As he pulled out of the driveway, Mo and I just looked at each other dumbfounded. What was that all about it? We thought God was going to meet our rent need? We're no better off now than before he came. In a split second the Lord showed me what happened. It was my pride. I should have been honest and told David about our desperate situation. After giving him enough time to get home, I called him and explained our true situation and asked if he could pay us back some of the money he owed. David replied, "Oh that explains everything. I felt a heaviness when I was with you guys, and I couldn't figure it out. To tell you the truth, we can't pay you back right now. But what I can do is mail you $300 as advance pay for helping me with that job, would that be alright?"

I told him that would be great, thanked him, hung up and praised God! Two days later, on the 28th, the check arrived and we dodged another bullet.

The next month my mother sent us a check for $1500 which carried us through July. But August was again another 'Perils of Pauline.' The Lord was still meeting our daily needs as they came up, but He was using these rents to really test our faith. This time He let us get down to the very last day. And this time we did much better.

On the last day of July, Joe and Sue came by to spend the day with us. That May, Sue had given birth to a beautiful blonde, blue-eyed girl who they name Shannon. The fact that "she" wasn't a "he" came as a surprise to us all, especially Joe, since the Lord had clearly told him He was giving him a son. But sometimes God speaks in parables, and hopefully one day we will understand the full meaning. The prophecy aside, they were thrilled with their gorgeous surprise from

God. And since she was a girl, Kathy was able to pass along all of her little girl's baby clothes, which blessed them immensely.

Shortly after moving into their rented house, Joe had landed a wonderful management job in a furniture company that was literally across the street from where they lived. All Joe had to do was walk down the driveway to go to work. It was God's perfect provision for their situation, since they only had one car. So God was blessing them, as well.

Soon it came time for them to leave. I asked if they'd pray with us for God to meet our rent, since it was due the following day. Standing in the driveway we all held hands, and with my eyes closed I began to praise and thank God for meeting all our needs and for supplying this month's rent. Suddenly I heard sobbing and opened my eyes to see it was Joe. Reaching for his handkerchief to blow his nose, he said through his sobs, "Sue, write them a check for the rent. How can I stand here with four hundred dollars in the bank, when my sister can't pay her rent?" Even though they didn't have much more than we did, God had moved on his heart to meet our need. We all started bawling then!

And so it went like that, month after month, for a whole year. Our mailbox, which was attached to a tree at the end of our driveway, became our lifeline as we hoped and prayed each day that a letter would arrive with manna from heaven. It didn't always come exactly when we wanted it, but it always came. According to Mo's diary, the Lord sent us over $11,000 that year thanks to the obedience and love of a whole lot of God's people.

All the way through this experience, the Lord was encouraging us to keep going and trust Him. One time when I was walking down the driveway crying out to Him about our situation, I looked up to see the ten-foot tall privet hedges behind the house transformed into the loving arms of God encircling and embracing our house. God was letting me know He was watching over and protecting my family, not to worry. The verse I clung to most during this time was, *"I have not seen the righteous forsaken, or his descendants begging bread"* (Ps. 37:25, NAS).

But as tough as it was to overcome fear and trust God to meet all our needs, that wasn't the hardest part. The hardest part, at least for me, was the daily struggle trying to justify why I wasn't working at some job. Any job. The inner voice accused me daily, "You haven't heard from God, You are just lazy. How could you let your family suffer like that?"

And if you are living in the midst of a hard-working community of farmers as we were, my unemployed status was like chalk on a blackboard. Plus, it was also a Bible-believing Christian community. And as any Christian can tell you, and probably will, the Bible is full of verses denouncing idleness. One verse, 2 Thessalonians 3:10, even says, *"If anyone will not work, neither let him eat" (NAS)*. Even an unbeliever knows not working isn't right.

God had to keep reminding me that this truly was not my doing, but His. I remember one day struggling with the guilt for not getting a job and opening my Bible to the Gospel of John and reading, *"DO NOT WORK FOR THE FOOD WHICH PERISHES, but for the food which endures to eternal life, which the Son of Man will give to you..."* (John 6:27 NAS). What a joy to hear the voice of the Lord confirm this to me, telling me to rest and not worry about working for a living right now. The guilt immediately vanished and my peace returned.

When all this first started to happen, it was roughest on Mo and I. Even though Mo was very supportive and never put pressure on me about it, she too wondered if we were doing the right thing or not. Who wouldn't? But one thing we couldn't deny—God was indeed meeting all our needs. As the saying goes, the proof is in the pudding.

However, after it was finally settled in our spirits it became rougher on those around us. Because the longer we went on having a daily need, the more pressure it put on folks to choose whether to meet it or not. If we were a family in crisis it would be one thing. But we were a family who had seemingly put ourselves in crisis and were doing nothing to try and resolve it. And that did not encourage someone to help us. It even made them feel like an enabler if they did.

Those closest to us, Kathy and Jerry and Joe and Sue and our other friends and relatives, I'm sure, had great difficulty accepting my behavior as justifiable. And who could blame them. If I were in their shoes, I'd have a problem with me also. Only their love and concern for us enabled them to overcome their growing discomfort with the whole situation. Although I realized all that, I could do nothing about it. I could only keep doing what I felt God telling me to do—and let the chips fall where they may.

I'd say the turning point for us came after the David Hunter episode. All the evidence pointed to the fact He was leading us to just rest in Him and let Him provide. But even after that miracle, I felt I still needed a clear word of confirmation. So I took the Little Champ and went up to a retreat center in the Poconos for a time of prayer and fasting. The center was situated in a beautiful 100-acre mountain setting that provided camper sites and offered great scenic solitude to get alone with God.

For the next two days I either prayed and read my Bible in the camper or walked through the wooded trails seeking to hear God's voice.

On the third day I wandered into the reception building, which was designed like a ski lodge. Iverna Tomkins, a well-known charismatic teacher, was speaking at the center that week. Thinking maybe I should talk to someone about my situation, I asked if they knew of any mature Christian leaders at the conference I could speak to. They suggested a husband and wife who were well known in local charismatic circles who were staying in a camper not far from mine.

Locating their camper, I knocked on the door. After a few minutes a man stuck his head out and asked what I wanted. I told him I was seeking some spiritual direction and that his name was given to me by the reception desk. Would he be willing to talk to me?

He invited me in and introduced me to his wife. The camper was poorly lit and I had the feeling they both had been resting and my visit was a bit unwelcome. But I was there now, so after a few introductions I launched into my story, starting with leaving my job in New York, going to school in Anaheim, leaving there at mid-term and coming here to Pennsylvania and now sitting on a farm waiting on God for direction. Did they have any suggestions?

They did. They started by grilling me with questions. How long was I reading my Bible each day? When I told them, they said that wasn't long enough for a minister in training. Brain surgeons study 14 hours a day. If I wanted to serve God, shouldn't I do at least that? They asked how much I prayed? Fasted? Meditated? Witnessed? When I failed all those questions they went on to tell me I had completely missed God. That I should have never left my job in New York. Never went to Melodyland—or left—or come here. And I certainly shouldn't be sitting on a farm doing nothing! I should be working!

When they had finished, I felt like I had been spiritually tarred and feathered and run out of town on a rail. Back in my camper I just held my head in my hands in a near panic. How could I have messed up so badly? How could I have left my job, sold our home and put my family in this terrible predicament? Worse, how was I going to tell Mo? As I imagined myself telling her, suddenly a light bulb came on. I heard Mo asking, "now *who* were these people who told you this?"

Oh, dear Lord! Yeah, who were these people? Immediately I understood I had just been broadsided by the enemy of my soul. And I started to get excited. If they were the lying voice of the enemy, than the exact opposite must be the truth. Which meant I was on the right track. I didn't screw up. God was with me!

I decided to head home immediately. Driving back I did a mental review of what had just happened. After discounting all the couple's bad advice, I had to admit they had one point: I probably should get a job. That's when I heard a calm voice of absolute certainty cut across my thoughts as clear as a bell, *"What do you think made them so angry?"*

I understood the Lord was telling me that my non-working status had convicted them of something. Which let me know in a reverse sort of way that there was something else going on with what God was doing with us than simply getting us to trust Him for our daily bread, as important as that was.

That revelation, which had to do with the Sabbath rest, came to light following another encounter with the established church.

Group photo: Pennsylvannia, 1978

Back row:
Joe, Sue, Jerry, Kathy, Brian, Mo,

Middle row:
Baby Shannon, Tara, Chris ,

Last row:
Brad, Becca, Todd, Brendan

Farm in Coopersburg, PA.
where we learned to live by faith.

Chapter 10

The Sabbath Rest

When we first arrived in Pennsylvania, we decided we'd better plug into one of the area churches. Kathy, having finally exited Catholicism, was attending a local Mennonite church, so we just went along with her. The event that had finally loosed Kathy from her commitment to Rome occurred while attending Mass one Sunday with her two children. Her four-year-old son, Brad, suddenly pointed to the large crucifix behind the altar and asked in a loud, horrified voice, "Mommy, why do they have a dead Jesus up there?" In that moment, Kathy heard the voice of God. Grabbing her kids by the hand, she said, "You're right Brad. Why do they have a dead Jesus up there? We're getting out of here."

Jerry, because of his commitment to the family restaurant, was still unable to do anything about church on Sunday. He was too busy cooking up breakfasts to feed the hundreds who stopped in after services.

We found in the Mennonite church a nice, quiet change of pace after all the California charismania. Over the following months we came to appreciate the simple, sincere lives of these spiritual descendants of the courageous Mennonite movement that arose in the Netherlands in the early 1500's. Named after a former Catholic priest, Menno Simons, Mennonites became the largest sect within the Anabaptist movement, which is the umbrella name given to all such groups who espoused believer's baptism over infant baptism. Because of that belief, they were brutally persecuted by both Catholic and Protestant leaders in

Europe. This caused many Mennonites to flee to America, a large contingent settling here in eastern Pennsylvania.

It wasn't long before the good folks in the church learned of my Bible college experience, abbreviated as it was, and invited me to teach one of the Bible study groups before the Sunday service. Since it gave me something to do besides just sit on the farm, I agreed. But in teaching the study, I quickly realized that as much as these people loved the Lord they were missing something—namely, the power of the Holy Spirit. I soon discovered why. The regional Mennonite Conference, to which this church belonged, had declared the Holy Spirit baptism with the evidence of speaking in tongues to be of the devil. So it was never promoted, because who would want to be possessed by the devil? Instead they believed a Christian received the Holy Spirit when he or she is born again, and that was it. There was no second blessing.

The pastor, who was a kind, loving man, knew about my charismatic Bible schooling but didn't let it interfere with our relationship. It was a— "don't ask, don't tell and don't speak in tongues around me"—sort of arrangement.

However, he wasn't opposed to another charismatic gift—healing. I learned that when he willingly prayed for me for a healing one day. Reading in my Bible one morning about Jesus healing the ten lepers, I felt the Holy Spirit nudge me concerning a chronic case of eczema on my fingers. I had contracted it having my hands in hot, soapy water cleaning glasses all the time when bartending at Cape Cod. The doctor told me it was incurable. I could only relieve the itching with ointment.

In the Bible story, after Jesus prayed for the lepers, He told them to go in faith and show themselves to the Jewish priests to be certified that they were indeed healed according to the Law of Moses. I felt the Lord tell me I too would be healed if I visited my "priest."

So off I went to see our Mennonite pastor. When I asked him to pray for my healing, he acknowledged that the Book of James did give us instructions for receiving such a manifestation. Taking his Bible, he confirmed his belief, reading, *"Is any one of you sick? He should call the elders of the church to pray over him and anoint him with oil in the name of the Lord. And the prayer offered in faith will make the sick person well"* (James 5:14,15). Providentially, the church's only other elder happened to be in the building that day besides the pastor. This elder, who was much older, was normally doing missionary work in some faraway jungle village. Sitting me in a chair, they poured a whole cruise of anointing oil on my head and prayed for my healing in the name of Jesus. As I was leaving, the older man smiled and said, "God bless you for your faith, son." Well one of them must have been in agreement with me, because three months later I was healed. I looked down one day and saw my fingers were completely clean of eczema. And remain so to this day. Praise the Lord!

Our comfortable relationship with this Mennonite church continued until one Sunday the pastor devoted his whole sermon to telling us why the power of the Sprit was not for the church today. He insisted such manifestations as tongues were something God only used to get the church up and running in the first century. After that, all such gifts disappeared. Therefore, those Christians who claimed to have received tongues today did not receive it from the Lord. He was too polite to say where he thought it did come from, but he didn't have to. Everyone knew.

I literally felt the Holy Spirit grieve within me at his words. So did Mo. And so did Kathy.

Following the service we all approached him and asked if we could speak with him. (These little meetings were becoming a habit with us.) We talked to him about the Baptism of the Holy Spirit for almost an hour, but he would not depart from his allegiance to the Mennonite playbook. So we finally told him we were sorry, but we couldn't continue to attend a church where the Holy Spirit wasn't welcome. He said he was sad to see us leave but he understood and we parted on good terms. We were told that his sermon the following week was about why people leave churches. He said it was because they want "to have their ears tickled." That is they only want to hear what they want to hear.

After this church exodus, we didn't feel pressured to rush out and join another one right away. Almost all the local believer churches in the area were Mennonite anyway, and now we knew where they stood. If we chose anything again, it would have to be charismatic—but not too charismatic. Since nothing within driving distance fit that profile, we decided to just sit tight for awhile.

But each Sunday morning, as we relaxed in our farmhouse setting, we would notice the cars hurrying down the road on their way to church services. It was that frantic activity, as contrasted to the peace we were enjoying, that prompted me to ask one day, "who's really resting on the Sabbath? Them or us? "

Soon I was digging through my Bible to find out what the Sabbath rest was really all about. I discovered it had nothing to do with Sunday, and everything to do with why we were sitting on this farm like two bumps on a log.

Almost all Christians know that the command *"to keep holy the Sabbath day"* is included in the Top Ten. And I think I can safely say most Christians believe they are obeying that Sabbath commandment by going to church on Sunday. I soon learned how far from the truth that notion was.

Among the many things the Protestant churches carried over from the Catholic Church was the teaching that the Saturday Sabbath, which is the Biblical Sabbath, had been changed under the New Covenant to Sunday. But when you search the New Testament, you will not find any Scriptural support for that belief. Just the opposite. The Scriptures were adamant that declaring any day a holy day requiring some kind of observance under the New Covenant is antithetical to having faith in Jesus. The same with saying that certain foods can't be eaten. All such religious legalisms nullify the completed work of Jesus, and constitute a gospel of works righteousness.

To the Colossians, Paul wrote, *"Therefore let no one act as your judge in regard to food or drink or in respect to a festival or a new moon or a Sabbath day– things which are a mere shadow of what is to come; but the substance belongs to Christ"* (Col. 2:16,17 NAS). If the substance is present, the shadow—or prototype—is no longer necessary.

To the Romans, Paul said, *"One man regards one day above another, another regards ever day alike. Let each man be fully convinced in his own mind"* (Rom. 14:5 NAS). If we want to set aside a personal day to the Lord we can, but there is no divine requirement to do so. The higher way of faith is to treat all days alike.

To the Galatians, who were backsliding into religious rules and regulations again, he wrote, *"...how is it that you turn back again to the weak and worthless elemental things, to which you desire to be enslaved all over again? You observe days and months and seasons and years. I fear for you, that perhaps I have labored over you in vain"* (Gal. 4:9-11, NAS).

I began to see that under the New Covenant there is no longer any commandment for God's people to keep a 24-hour day Sabbath as under the Old Covenant. Like the rest of the legal commands of the Mosaic Law, it was retired, having been fulfilled in Jesus. So where did this Sunday observance originate? You guessed it. From the same early churchmen who started transitioning the Jewish religion into a Gentile religion, never fully understanding that Jesus had transitioned us into no religion at all. But into a living relationship with the Godhead.

This time the leaven came from a church father named Justin Martyr, who first described and then justified a growing custom of Sunday worship among gatherings of early Christians: "We hold our common assembly on the Sun's Day because it is the first day on which God put to flight darkness and chaos and made the world; and on the same day Jesus Christ our Savior rose from the dead; for they crucified him on the day before Saturn's day, on the Sun's day, which follows Saturn's..." (Apologia I; lxvii).

Eventually, the Emperor Constantine offically decreed the Sun's Day to be the official Sabbath day of the Christian religion, later termed 'the Lord's Day.' And this decree continues in effect today, enforced by the power of tradition, but not by the Word of God.

In turning the Jewish Sabbath into a Christian holy day of obligatory worship, church leaders missed the central concept behind the Sabbath. The root of the word "Sabbath" comes from *shabbat* – a Hebrew word meaning "to cease" (Strongs Concordance, #7673). When God gave Moses the fourth commandment about the Sabbath, He based it on the seventh day of the creation story in Genesis when God rested after six days of work. The idea was not for man to do something religious on that day, like go to church—but to stop all manual labor and rest in the rest of God. Which is why Jesus said *"the Sabbath was made for man, not man for the Sabbath"* (Mark 2:27).

I saw then that Jesus was indeed the fulfillment of the Sabbath Day. In Him alone can we enter God's rest and thereby fulfil this commandment today. If the First Covenant Sabbath provided a day of physical rest, the New Covenant Sabbath provided a "day" of spiritual rest. But I also saw that this spiritual rest had two aspects to it, which explained why the Lord had us sitting there on Sunday while people drove to church, and then sitting there the rest of the week while people drove to work.

The first rest is a rest from all our efforts to seek favor with God and receive His reward of righteousness. That is we can rest from all religious activity and the mindset that our works will earn us salvation or sanctification or God's favor. Including doing "good things" like going to a church on Sunday. Scripture teaches that we have already been reckoned righteous through faith in Jesus (2 Cor 5:21). It is a free gift that cannot be earned. The idea that it could be earned wasn't even true under the Old Covenant. But because Israel was required to keep the laws of Moses the people got confused and thought righteousness was tied to their religious performance. It wasn't. *"...but Israel, pursuing a law of righteousness, did not arrive at that law. Why? Because they did not pursue it by faith, but though it were by works"* (Rom 9:31,32 NAS).

Under the New Covenant we have no religion to confuse us—or we shouldn't have—and so we can rest more easily from all notions of works righteousness. *"But to the one who does not work (for salvation) but believes in Him* who justifies the ungodly, his faith is reckoned as righteousness..." (Rom. 4:5 NAS) This 'rest for the spirit' I call the Passover rest, which is fulfilled in us when we are born again.

The second aspect of this Sabbath rest is 'a rest for the soul.' It delivers us from all the emotional anxiety connected to human endeavor, including striving to earn a living. This is why the camper couple got so upset with me. They were being convicted of putting working for a living ahead of obedience to God. Obedience is God's first priority. It even takes precedence over getting a job. *"This is the work of God, that you believe in Him whom He has sent"* (John 6:29 NAS).

What do I mean when I say we don't have to strive to earn a living? It's what Jesus was saying in his often quoted sermon about not being anxious about trying to provide for ourselves. He pointed to the birds that neither sow nor reap, yet our Heavenly Father feeds them. And the lillies of the field that neither toil nor spin, but yet are dressed more regally than King Solomon ever was. In fact, He said that the only ones who need to worry about such things as food, clothing and shelter are the unbelievers. Not believers. *"But seek first the Kingdom of God and His righteousness; and all these things will be added to you"* (Matt 6:25-34 NAS).

In other words, we don't have to worry about trying to provide for ourseves anymore. He takes the responsibilty for making sure we are well taken care of when we enter His rest by faith. Which means we are always guaranteed employment and a great benefits package? He is our source for everything. So why worry? As Jesus said, *"Come to Me, all you who are weary and heavy laden, and I will give you rest. Take my yoke upon you, and learn from Me, for I am gentle and humble of heart; and you shall find rest for your souls. For my yoke is easy, and my load is light"* (Matt 11:28-30 NAS). And lest there be any doubt He is talking about Himself as the fulfillment of the Sabbath, a few verses later He declares Himself, *"Lord of the Sabbath"* (12:8).

That doesn't mean we won't have to do physical labor ever again, or work hard for an employer, but rather our preservation no longer depends upon our own strength and ingenuity. But rather upon our willingness to trust Him to meet all our needs. That means we no longer work for whoever we work for, but for Jesus, knowing His work is not burdensome. That's because He is the only Boss we will ever have who insists on doing all the work Himself. *"The One who calls you is faithful, and he will do it"* (1 Theses. 5:24). It's a supernatural work and therefore requires supernatural ability. It will be done through us, but not by us, *"...but by My Spirit,' says the Lord Almighty"* (Zech. 4:6).

This 'rest of the soul' I call the rest of Pentecost, which we can enter into by faith through the enabling of the Baptism of the Holy Spirit.

There is a third Sabbath rest that is linked to the third and final Israelite pilgrimage feast, the Feast of Tabernacles, or Succoth. This one we have not appropriated yet, but it is about to be revealed. I believe it's the rest the writer of Hebrews is referring to when he says, *"There remains, then, a Sabbath-rest for the people of God"* (Heb 4:9). It is the rest that was forfeited by our forefathers when they refused to go into the Promised Land under Moses. We are told that Joshua didn't bring them into that rest either, but that it was postponed to a future date. I believe this rest will deliver us from all fear of war, terror and bodily harm, including sickness and disease and old age. It will be a rest for the body. But we won't know the full extent of this blessing until it appears.

So the spiritual principle foreshadowed in the fourth commandment is that God wants us to cease from all "works of the flesh" to try and secure or save ourselves. It is not about physical labor and how little or how much we sweat. Or about this calendar day or that one. It's about resting in the finished work of Jesus. The work is done and He is seated now at the right hand of the Father (Eph. 1:20). He is at rest. He is the Sabbath Day. Watchman Nee, in his classic work, Sit, Walk, Stand, contrasts how at creation God worked for six days and rested on the seventh. But man, who was created on the sixth day, started his work life in the day of God's rest. So we see that man must first enter God's rest before he can work. Which means, ironically, the Sabbath Day is the only day we can really work. Because the work done in and through Him is simply the bringing forth of the work He has already accomplished. And that is the only work that glorifies God.

The prophet Isaiah described it best: *"If because of the Sabbath, you turn your foot from doing your own (religious or secular) pleasure on My holy day, and call the Sabbath a delight the holy day of the Lord honorable, and shall honor it, desisting from your own ways, and seeking your own pleasure, and speaking your own word, then you will take delight in the Lord, and I will make you ride on the heights of the earth, and I will feed you with the heritage of Jacob your father, for the mouth of the Lord has spoken"* (Isa. 58:13,14 NAS).

Learning about the Sabbath rest and discovering that God will meet all our needs, was the major revelation we received on the farm. However, being shown something and being able to walk in it with any consistency are two different things. As you will quickly see demonstrated in the next chapter.

FLEECE

Brian Hennessy

As the corn grew taller and then tasseled and then disappeared into the harvester, we realized winter was returning and our year lease would soon expire. Although the farmer graciously offered to extend it for another six months, we declined. We'd learned his wife had been diagnosed with a serious cancer, and with the barn now completed, we figured they were probably looking forward to moving into the house.

We started praying about where we should go next. I soon sensed the Lord leading us to return to our roots in Connecticut. Specifically, Bristol, Connecticut, a town where we'd never been before. Since this would entail another major move, Mo and I needed to be sure I'd heard correctly. We decided to use Mo's engagement ring as the sign. About six months before, Mo had decided that her beautiful two-carat diamond ring that she loved dearly was a little incongruous with our new lifestyle. And since we could sure use the money, she suggested we try and sell it. After locating a trustworthy jewler in Allentown who assured us he could find a buyer, we'd left it with him. But in the months that followed, the ring still had not sold. So as a confirmation that we were to go to Bristol, Connecticut, we asked the Lord to sell the ring within seven days. We said nothing to the jeweler.

On the last day of our "fleece," I got a surprise call from our jewler friend to inform me he'd met a rabbi at a New York trade show who "showed some interest in the piece," as he put it. But he'd heard nothing since. While he's telling me this, he suddenly excuses himself to take a call on another line, would I hold? He was gone for a good thirty seconds, and when he returns he says with amazement,

"Guess what? That was the rabbi! He definitely wants the stone. If we'll bring it to New York next week, he'll buy it."

So we had our sign. And after going up to New York the following week we also had the money we needed to relocate to the Nutmeg state. The downside to all this, of course, was leaving Joe and Sue and Kathy and Jerry behind. We had been meeting regularly together for Bible study and fellowship and I felt like we were abandoning them. But the Lord was moving us on, so I simply had to commit them to His care and realize they at least had each other.

So in God's perfect timing, one year from the day we moved into the farmhouse, we moved out. We left the camper parked in Jerry's barn and packed all our furniture and stuff into a rental truck. While I drove the truck with my son Chris, Mo followed in the station wagon with the other kids.

Another wild faith adventure lay ahead.

Chapter 11

Joy Comes in the Morning

By the time we reached Bristol, we were a three-car, one-truck caravan. We had been joined by my brother Neil and Pat and their four girls, as well as by David Hunter and his wife, Jill, the friend who had helped us that first month on the farm. They all lived in nearby towns and were as curious as we were to see what miracle God was going to provide this time.

Bristol, as we soon discovered, was an old, manufacturing town with lots of red brick buildings that once housed industries long since forced into retirement. You sensed it was a town in transition, struggling to free itself from the past and discover new ways to prosper. It didn't exactly give us a warm, encouraging feeling.

Since we didn't have a clue where we were supposed to go, we simply drove around the town looking for some sign from heaven. As the day wore on and we received no word or direction from God, the Hunters finally invited us back to their place to spend the night. Leaving the truck in a school parking lot, we followed the Hunters to their home, about a half hour away. Although they had four kids of their own, there was still enough room in their spacious ranch house to fit us all.

The next morning it was decided that the wives and kids would remain at the house, while David and I would continue the search in Bristol. When another day of circling about proved fruitless, we returned again to David's house for a second night.

In the morning, David and Jill came to us and said that God had spoken to them: we were supposed to live with them. They told us that six months before the Lord had led them to fix up their downstairs basement apartment because He was going to send someone to live with them. They just never thought it would be us until last night.

To be honest, I wasn't thrilled by the idea. I had hoped for our own quarters and an environment more conducive to starting the ministry the Lord had promised me. Whatever it was. I asked them to give me a few minutes while I went and prayed about this. I was hoping the Lord would say no, but when I opened my Bible and started reading, I came to this verse: *"Weeping may last for the night, but a shout of joy comes in the morning"* (Ps.30:5 NAS). It being morning, I felt the Lord saying I'd better start shouting and thanking Him—and the Hunters, too. In case I hadn't noticed, there were no other offers on the table. I got the message.

So we said yes, thanked David and Jill for doing this for us, and moved in.

As it turned out, the Lord had provided quite adequately, as always. Their above ground basement, which had it's own outside entrance, provided the perfect amount of space to fit us all. There was a small private bedroom for Mo and I, a full bathroom, a little carpeted living room with a fireplace with room for a TV and sofa, a kitchen bar area where we could cook and eat, and a large playroom area that we turned into a dormitory for the kids. My brother-in-law, Joe, had given us some room-dividers before leaving Pennsylvania, which were just what we needed to give the kids some privacy. All the furniture that we didn't need or couldn't fit, we stacked in the garage. We were in, snug as a bug in a rug. Praise the Lord!

Since David had his own security alarm business, it was decided that I'd be his first employee. Our living quarters would be provided rent free and they'd pay me a hundred dollars a month to work as David's assistant. Though I didn't have a clue about electronics, David said he could teach me all I needed to know. I had already worked one job with him back in Pennsylvania, so I had a little experience. Mostly I'd be stringing wire and mounting electronic gadgets, while David figured out what devices to install and where to put them. As I found out, he was a genius at home protection.

While I began my new career in electronics, Mo stayed at the house with Jill. Altogether there were four adults and eight children, including the Hunter's newborn baby girl. All our children, except Todd, were quickly registered into the local schools with the Hunter kids and within a few weeks our new life was starting to take on its own rhythm and flow. As David had promised, I started to get the hang of things and I enjoyed our time together and solving each new installation. Mo and Jill and the kids were all getting along well, also.

Like us, the Hunters had been Catholics. They were former neighbors of my brother Neil in New Fairfield, Connecticut before moving to this house. When we had our awakening it created a kind of domino effect that first hit Neil and Pat, and through them, a number of other Catholic families on their street, including the Hunters. So they were well aware of our story and had been following us closely, never expecting to find themselves in the middle of that story one day.

After leaving the Catholic Church, the Hunters had checked out of institutional religion altogether. So we became part of their church in the home. We didn't meet regularly, but we were always sharing Bible insights and praying together. But as time went on, Mo and I started to crave our privacy more and more, limited as it was, so our fellowship and communication began to diminish. Which, in retrospect, was a mistake we made.

That summer, the temperatures soared into the high nineties. It was one of the hottest summers ever in Connecticut. The linoleum floor in our apartment began to sweat, dirt and mildew began to settle on our stuff in the garage, and we could hear mice running through the ductwork over our heads at night. Plus, all the kids were now home for summer vacation.

David and I could escape to work during the day, but the wives and the kids were always in the house. With money in short supply, Mo couldn't go shopping or drive around much. Fortunately, the Hunters had a lot of wooded property behind their house where the kids could play. But the walls were starting to close in on us.

What really made things difficult, however, was when the Hunter's 16-year-old nephew moved in. He had had a difficult home situation and eventually got into some trouble. It was either go to reform school or move in with his uncle David. Although basically a nice kid, he was undisciplined and soon started antagonizing the younger children. That only added to our growing discomfort.

But the dynamic that was really frustrating me the most was that with each passing week, my hopes and dreams of entering ministry seemed to be drifting further out of reach. "Lord, how much longer? Is this what I left my advertising career for? What happened to my life's calling?" became my daily SOS. I knew the Lord had led us into this situation, and only He could lead us out. We had crawled too far out on the limb to find our way back down. I wouldn't even know where to begin.

For awhile my pea brain thought that maybe the Lord was truly giving me a new career, and I would partner with David and we'd become prosperous together and launch into ministry together. That thought came to a crashing halt when he sent me out on my first solo job, a so-called "two-hour piece of cake" to install a simple door buzzer in a brain surgeon's office. Four hours later I was still in there sweating profusely trying to get the door buzzer to work as the surgeon's frail, often bandaged patients picked their way around my tools which were now spread all over the entrance foyer. Finally, I had to call David to come rescue me. As it turned out it wasn't all my fault. The buzzer was a dud.

Nevertheless, it convinced me that electronics was not my calling. But instead of faithfully fulfilling my duties with a smile until God moved us on, I began to emotionally disengage from the work. My thoughts were only of getting out of this job and my family somewhere else. And as my despair deepened, I sensed David was starting to have the same thoughts about us, as well.

What I didn't fully understand at the time was the Lord's process of sanctification, which requires breaking the power of the carnal nature in us before He can use us for anything. I'm sure I'd heard that taught somewhere, but when it became my flesh that was being squeezed, all abstract teaching on the subject evaporated immediately. And as I eventually discovered to my dismay, beneath the surface of my normally easy-going personality, I had a strong carnal will that wasn't about to lie down without a fight. But I also discovered His loving hand is well able to bring *"everything into conformity with the purpose of His will"* (Eph 1:11). But it is a painful process. Death always is.

One day, in total desperation over our situation, I cried out with a plea for help that I knew penetrated the heavens. And the joy that immediately filled my heart communicated His answer was, *"Yes, I will bring you out before the start of school in September."* Moving before the kids started another school year was a big part of our concern. We knew if we didn't leave before September we'd be stuck here for another year because it would be too disruptive for the kids to make another mid-year school move. This school was now there sixth one in three years. So I knew that God's "Yes!" included the school thing.

I quickly told Mo and the kids that the Lord had assured me we'd be someplace else by the start of September. Everybody was happy to hear that. Knowing the end was in sight even allowed me to get my head and emotions back into my job with David. Later, I determined the date of the 24th of August would be the day of our coming miracle. I'm not sure how I arrived at that number, but it quickly became my lighthouse on the distant shore.

The 24th finally came. It was a Saturday. The Hunters planned to visit some relatives that weekend and were leaving us in charge of the business. Besides installing security devices, the Hunters would also monitor them. That meant someone had to be there 24-hours a day, in case of a break-in. So we were glad, at least, that we could be there to let them get away occassionally.

We'd told David and Jill of our deliverance date, and by now they were looking forward to it as much as we were. After telling us they'd be back late on Sunday, they left us alone with our hope.

The day moved along quickly. Too quickly. Before I knew it, the sun was going down and nothing had happened yet. I was trying to hold onto my faith, but I could feel it crumbling. When it got to be 10 o'clock, my faith became fear. I'd pinned so much on this deliverance, that I began to get angry at God for what was starting to look like a failed promise. How could God do this to me? Walking out on the deck, I shook my fist at the heavens, and told God that if He didn't deliver us, I was going to hang a big sheet on the front of the house saying, "God fails!" That's how far gone I was. Thankfully, the Lord is full of compassion and knows the weakness of our flesh, or else I'd probably be toast now.

When the clock struck midnight without a sign from heaven, my hopes were dashed. But by now I was too exhausted to even comtemplate the consequences of God's no-show. I flopped down on the couch next to Mo who was handling the whole thing a lot better than I. We would have dragged ourselves to bed at this point except we had to wait for one of David's monitored clients, a pizza parlor, to close at one o'clock. Since we had to stay up anyway, we flipped on the TV to numb the pain.

The Johnny Carson show came on. But the host that night was someone else standing in for the vacationing Johnny, and his first guest was Pat Boone. We felt a slight bit of encouragement because we knew Pat was a Christian. And that encouragement grew when we recognized his first song to be an old Christian favorite. But then a very unusual thing occurred. In the middle of the song Pat forgot the words. He tried faking it for a few stanzas, but finally gave up and returned to his seat by the host. Apologizing profusely, Pat explained that he'd sung the song for so many years he didn't think he needed cue cards. So once he'd lost it he couldn't recover. He said that was the first time anything like that had ever happened to him.

Valley of the Steeples

By now Mo and I were so absorbed in Pat's troubles that we completely forgot about our own. The host ribbed him about it, saying it was audition night, inviting anyone with a song to come on down. Finally, tongue in cheek, he asked Pat if he had another song he'd like to try out. Glad for the chance to redeem himself, Pat said he did and stepped to the mike and began to sing, <u>Tomorrow</u>, the title song from the hit Broadway play, <u>Annie.</u>

As the camera zoomed in for a close-up of Pat's smiling face, we suddenly heard Jesus singing to us, *"The sun'll come out tomorrow... so you gotta hang on 'til tomorrow, come what may. Tomorrow! Tomorrow! I love ya! Tomorrow! You're <u>only</u> a day a way!* " (Although the actual lyric Pat sang was "always," we heard "only.")

I looked at Mo to see if she was hearing what I was hearing. She was. We both knew Jesus was telling us to hold on until tomorrow, the miracle would come tomorrow. Not today, tomorrow!

Immediately the heaviness in both our hearts lifted and was replaced by an incredible joy. The Lord had waited until I had exhausted every bit of human strength before keeping His word to me. How could I have ever doubted? Hadn't I learned anything on the farm? Oh, the flesh is such a faith-eating thing. When the pizza store finally closed we went to bed with high hopes for what tomorrow would bring.

In the morning we gathered the kids together in the living room and told them what had happened the night before. They, of course, had been waiting for the miracle also. We explained that we didn't know when it would happen, but sometime today. While we were all sitting there the phone rang. I got up and answered it. It was Mo's sister Kathy callling from Pennsylvania. She just wanted to tell us about a wild and crazy dream she had last night

Not knowing anything about our desire to escape our present situation and move into our own home, Kathy related her dream to me. She shared how she saw us all living in a large house that belonged to some friends of hers, the Lupinaccis, down there in Pennsylvania. She said the dream was so real, that even after a visit to the bathroom, it resumed when she went back to bed.

"Kathy," I said, realizing her dream was the start of our miracle,"that was the Lord!"

"Oh, no, I don't think so, Brian. It was just a dream…but it was strange."

"No, listen to me, Kathy," I said. "We are all sitting here waiting for a word from the Lord to tell us where to move and you called to tell us about this strange dream of us being in a house. It is definitely the Lord!"

"Do you really think so?"

"Absolutely! Trust me, it's the Lord"

"Well, funny thing, their house is for sale. I believe they are supposed to move to some Caribbean island soon to manage a hotel but they haven't been able to sell the house."

"Kathy, call them and see if they'd like to rent it to us," I suggested.

She said she would and then get back to me.

An hour later she called again to say the Lupinaccis would indeed rent it to us. They said in ten days we could move in, and that we were an answer to prayer. We both had received a miracle! I don't know what the Lupinaccis did on their end, but the Hennessys all let out a whoop of joy. Later I remembered the Scripture the Lord gave me when we first came to the Hunters that encouraged me to move in: *"Weeping lasts for the night, but joy comes in the morning."*

Valley of the Steeples

I realized now that verse was more of a prophecy about our departure than our arrival.

When Kathy told us the Lupinacci's would rent it to us for $450, I quickly agreed. But the truth was it wouldn't have mattered to me if they had said $2000 a month, I would have said yes. That's how badly I wanted out of that basement. Plus, I knew if the Lord was leading us there, the money would be there, too.

That very day we started to pack. All we knew about the Lupinacci house so far was that it was large and had a barn with five acres of land. Kathy kept describing it as a "Greenwich house," referring to the grand-style homes we were familiar with in Greenwich, Connecticut. So we figured it couldn't be too shabby.

The first thing I did after Kathy's call was to dig out an old bed sheet and write on it, GOD <u>NEVER</u> FAILS! I hung it over the garage doors in atonement for my unbelief, and that was the first thing the Hunters saw when they came home.

Later we wrote to Pat Boone to tell him how God had used him to sing us a message of hope and deliverance. He wrote back thanking us for clearing up the mystery of one of the most embarassing moments of his career. He said it reminded him once again that *"God works all things together for good to those who love God, to those who are called according to His purpose"* (Rom. 8:28). We treasure his letter as a reminder of the miracle God did for us that day.

Chapter 12

The Last Church

It was a wonderful feeling as we turned into Kathy and Jerry's long, tree-lined driveway again. Joe and Sue were also there to greet us. Everyone was so happy to have us back in Pennsylvania. And we were so glad to be back. It was a true home coming.

Knowing we were eager to see our new home, Kathy got into her car and told us to follow her. She'd lead us to the Lupinacci house, which was about a half-hour south in a small town called Telford.

After twisting and turning her way through the back roads, Kathy finally pulled into a wide, gravel driveway in front of a large, white, three-story house with a separate two-car garage. I remember thinking as we followed her in that this is not what I'd call a "Greenwich house." Mo later told me she had the very same first impression. The house, as we soon learned, was a Victorian-style farmhouse. Square shaped, it had lots of porches and balconies with gingerbread trim to give it character and appeal. But it looked a bit tired in need of a fresh coat of paint.

As we parked, I spotted an in-the-ground swimming pool in an enclosed patio area, for which I silently praised the Lord! But the dominating structure on the property was a huge red barn with a silver roof and silo. The property itself was divided up into lawn on one side of the driveway. And on the other side, a two-acre fenced-in pasture, where a palomino pony, several sheep, a goat and a couple of geese grazed.

Climbing out of our cars, we were greeted by the entire Lupinacci family who had been waiting in the driveway to welcome us. Kathy introduced us to them. The wife's name was Maureen, the same as Mo's, and his name was Richard. They had four children, just as we did, all about the same ages as our kids. They quickly told us how they were scheduled to leave for the island of Nevis in a few days, and how glad they were we were moving into their house. We all agreed that only God could have put this together.

We then went inside. If the outside of the house wasn't all we expected, the inside was everything we could hope for. Passing through the large eat-in country kitchen we entered a large living room with high ceilings, bay windows, hardwood floors with two beautiful oriental rugs, and a baby grand piano. A dining room, sitting room and powder room completed the first floor.

Upstairs we found five good-sized bedrooms and two more baths. The master and one other bedroom even had a walkout balcony. On the third floor were five more rooms, but they were unusable except for storage.

Maureen and Richard told us they were leaving all the beds, the furniture, the pictures—even the sheets and towels, which were presently in the dryer. We were thrilled to hear that, because the place was so big we didn't have enough furniture to fill it. Richard told me he'd even leave his 48-inch ride-around mower for us, also.

The whole thing felt a little bizarre. Like we were taking over their lives as they moved on to a new assignment from God. Tara later said, sitting on her bed in front of her own dresser in her own room again, "Now I really know there is a God!" We'd gone from a basement to all this with one dream within ten days! What a God we serve!!

The house also confirmed in spades a promise the Lord had given Mo before we left Stamford, Connecticut: *"Let me assure you that no one has ever given up anything – home, brothers, sisters, mother, father, children or property – for love of me and to tell others the Good News, who won't be given back a hundred times over, homes, brothers, sisters mothers, children, and land – with persecutions"* (Mark 10:29, 30 LB).

With our own home again, we felt we had gotten our lives back. But now what? Do I get a job? Do we go back to trusting the Lord to provide? We were now that much closer to Philadelphia where there were probably some good-sized ad agencies. So Mo and I prayed, "Lord show us what to do." We still had a couple of hundred dollars from working for the Hunters, but that wouldn't last long.

I decided to test the waters. Digging out my porfolio of ads, I visited a large, manufacturing business in the area that I figured must have an advertising department. They did, and after graciously agreeing to interview me they said they'd let me know. Well, they didn't waste any time. Before I got home from the interview they had called and told Mo, sorry, my application had been turned down. The rejection was so swift that I felt the Lord was sending me a message. So I went up to the barn and began to talk to God in earnest about it. As I paced about inside the barn praising God and seeking direction, suddenly the Lord gave me a vision. Just as it happened with Mo, the barn interior diasappeared and I was looking close-up at the base of a massive office building where it joined the sidewalk. I had the sense I'd seen this before. Later I realized the Lord had used an early childhood experience to speak to me. My father had taken me into New

York City once as a small boy and we had passed this same building. I commented that it was so dirty they should tear it down. My father just chuckled and said, "look up!" It was the Empire State Building.

In the vision, a pair of hands appeared and slid under the sky scraper and easily lifted it off the ground like it was made of balsa wood. I gasped, "Lord, that's impossible!" And instantly the vision vanished.

Joy flooded my soul as I understood what the Lord was saying. He was telling me the work He'd called me to do was a certainty. It would take place. I'd just seen it represented by the lifting of the building. It was a work so impossible that only God could do it, so don't even think about attempting it in my own strength.

I understood also that He was telling me to cease all worrying about "the ministry." It would take place in the future in God's timing. Instead I was to rest in Him and just focus on doing whatever He sent along for me to do. And then do it with all my might. Oh, how I wish I could say I followed that simple set of instructions to the letter, and that everything was lovely after that. Unfortunately, I would disobey the Lord again, and this time the Lord would not overlook my actions as He did at the Hunters. I would be severely disciplined for it. But then I'm getting ahead of the story.

I should mention that a few months later, while watching television, a real estate company's commercial came on that began with almost the exact same scene as the vision of the Empire State Building. A pair of hands slid under a house foundation and started to lift it up. As the camera pulled back, it revealed the house ringed by many agents who were helping to lift it—i.e. helping you sell your home. I realized it was a confirmation from the Lord about what He'd shown me, and informing me at the same time that I wouldn't be alone in this work. That many would help in "lifting" this impossible load. Which I now strongly suspect stands for lifting the Ecclesiastical Empire State Building off the backs of God's people and setting them free to follow the Lord.

Leaving the barn, I was absolutely euphoric. I had heard from heaven and felt I was right on track with God's plan. Over the next few days I would discover that in the process God had imparted to me a new authority and a new confidence. I felt more decisive than I had ever felt in my life. And I had more energy. I also discovered I had gained greater spiritual insight. I started teaching some of the most anointed Bible lessons of my life after that. But within a few weeks it all seemed to fade away. I'm still not sure if it just became part of me, like a computer upgrade. Or if it was a taste of things to come?

Although I hadn't gotten a direct answer from God concerning what kind of work I should be doing now, I knew at least I was not to worry about it. The work would come. My only concern now was telling Mo. I knew she was anxious to get back to some kind of normal living, and that included me getting a regular paycheck. How could I tell her God said I wasn't to go job hunting, but that the work would come to me? We needed money now! So I asked God for some confirmation. "Lord," I prayed, "show Mo that I really did hear from you about this work thing by providing a financial blessing in the next seven days." Sensing I had a deal, I told Mo that the check was in the mail. And she was fine with that. We would wait and see.

While all this was going on, developments were also stirring on the church front. A couple of weeks earlier we'd learned of an exciting charismatic fellowship in the area that was meeting in a school auditorium. We heard they were mostly Mennonites who had received the Baptism of the Holy Spirit and no longer felt comfortable or welcome in their denominational churches. It sounded like the perfect blend of spiritual power and Scripture-wise Mennonite maturity we were looking for. It had been over a year since we had been in a church, and although I can't say we missed it terribly, we still felt we needed to be part of a body. Plus, we were anxious to meet other believers in the area. So we paid them a visit.

Our first impressions were good. Lots of great worship songs, microphone sharing from the congregation, a warm sense of community and a wonderful group of people who truly were alive in the Lord. I was excited that maybe here at last we would find a fresh wind of freedom.

The senior pastor wasn't present the first two weekends we attended, but the assistant pastor did a great job of teaching, I thought. On our second visit one of the couples in the congregation even took us to lunch after the service to get to know us better. Since this was the day after I had asked God for a financial miracle, I thought maybe the Lord was going to use them. But He didn't.

As the week went by, I continued to wait on God with great hope for my financial sign. But by the following Saturday, which was the last day, we were down to ten dollars and no time left on the calendar. I kept trying to reassure Mo that the Lord would do *something*. And she trusted me. Or rather God. That night I lay awake in bed until midnight hoping against hope that He would still do something miraculous as He had done at the Hunters. Refusing to despair, as I had done at the Hunters, I just kept speaking quietly to Him from my heart telling Him I trusted Him no matter what. And that I knew He would not fail me.

Suddenly the Lord began to speak to me.

"In church tomorrow, stand up and tell everyone you have a financial need."

My heart almost stopped. Not because God was speaking to me, but because I could see myself standing up and telling all those people who we barely knew that we needed money.

"Why would they listen to me, Lord?" I asked. "They don't know me."

"Tell them your testimony," came the confidence-building reply. *"If you tell them your testimony, they will get to know you and they will listen to you."*

I couldn't believe I was actually having an extended conversation with God. I'd read about other believers experiencing this, but here it was happening to me. As I thought about the Lord's answer, it made sense. Knowing the instructions came from the Lord gave me the courage to do it. I finally drifted off asleep thinking that something really good was going to happen tomorrow.

The next morning we took our seats in the auditorium. I noticed someone new standing up front, and guessed it was the senior pastor who'd been absent the first two weeks. I hadn't said anything to Mo about my midnight chat with the Lord, or about what I was intending to do. If she knew, I figured, it would make her a nervous wreck and she'd probably try to talk me out of it. Which at that moment wouldn't be too hard to do.

After the congregation sang a few songs of praise and worship, a mike was passed around to anyone who had a prayer request or a testimony to share about a recent blessing from God. Knowing my story was going to take awhile, I waited until everyone had spoken. When the time for sharing was over, the pastor had us all stand as he prayed, and then asked us to be seated. But when everyone else sat down, I remained standing. Noticing me, and sensing I had something to say, the pastor asked that a mike be brought over to me. I was grateful for that because everything said through the mike was recorded and later I was able to get an audio tape of my whole sharing.

After introducing myself, I did as the Lord instructed. I stated that we had a financial need, and asked if I might share our testimony so they could learn more about us. The pastor gave me permission to proceed so I launched into our whole testimony, starting from our leaving Connecticut, going to California and right up to that very minute. It took almost an hour to tell the whole story.

When I finished, the pastor said he had been praying asking God what he should do. He then instructed me to come down front and to be given one of their collection buckets. Turning to the congregation, he then invited anyone who wished to, to come forward and contribute something to our need. Holy humbling experience! Since it was too late to run, which both my legs were telling me to do, I went down front as he instructed. He handed me a white, plastic bucket and I turned around to await the benevolence of the congregation.

What I saw made my eyes fill with tears. The entire church was empting out of their seats and streaming down to the front. A line formed and hands began dropping dollars and checks into the bucket. There were whispers of promised dinners to come. And hugs and tears. One lady said the Lord had told her to go back for more money as she was leaving for church. Another said they'd been praying for a spiritual breakthrough in the church and felt this was it. Pretty soon the bucket was filled and they brought me another one.

After everyone returned to their seats I was left standing there in a daze with two full buckets overflowing with God's blessings. But the Lord had one more surprise. The pastor confessed that he'd come there that morning without a sermon. He even had people praying for him to get a message, but had drawn a blank. So he too had come by faith that morning, trusting God to provide. My sharing had been God's provision for him as well. We'd both been obedient and the Lord had rewarded us.

When we got home we dumped both buckets on the kitchen table. The kids thought it was the neatest thing they'd ever seen. The amount totaled over $1700. But what made it even more meaningful was that all the money was given *after* the regular collection had been taken.

Since we didn't feel it was right to just take the money and run, we returned the following Sunday. And the next. And soon we were part of the congregation. Which was fine. We were enjoying the services and it was nice to feel part of a body again. But as time went on, our initial excitement about this church began to wane. Not that the preaching, singing and fellowship weren't good, they were. It was just that we expected to see something different in this church, and we didn't.

To explain what I mean, let me use the American Revolution as an analogy. After America broke free from British colonial rule, our forefathers quickly set up a new government reflective of the principles and ideals they had fought so valiantly to acquire. But imagine if they hadn't. Suppose they had simply recreated the same kind of government they had just rejected? One that enthroned a king, favored taxation without representation, and made the Church of England our national church to name a few things.

The people would have risen up in arms again and said, "What are you nuts?!"

We knew this group had broken loose from the Mennonite Church, so I guess we expected those called to leadership in this band of 'escapees' to reorganize differently. That their approach to church life would be gentler, based more on the biblical model of mutual submission. That they would recognize each believer had a unique calling and ministry that was vital to the growth of the body. And that the leadership would reflect more of a servanthood nature. But it was the same old church system again, just done with more energy. They still relied on the old hierarchical form of government with its top-down rule of authority. Still continued to perpetuate a clergy mentality that saw the congregation as "laity." Still saw the people as their people, not God's people. And although nobody was telling the new government they were nuts, grumblings of discontent were definitely beginning to surface. I just don't think anybody, including us, could quite put their finger on what was wrong and articulate it. But there was a familiar smell of death in the air.

From the start, Mo and I felt a certain coolness towards us coming from the top leadership. It felt like we were being watched more than we were being loved, especially by the senior pastor. It got to the point where I finally asked to meet with him privately and told him about my "paranoia." He was honest enough to admit there was some truth to it and apologized. But even so, things didn't improve all that much afterwards. I suspect we were a bit of an enigma to them. Even though we were doctrinally on the same page concerning the baptism of the Holy Spirit, we were from different religious and cultural backgrounds. Plus, I don't think our dramatic fund-raising event helped, either.

Another thing we suspect didn't help was that we were holding a Bible study at our house unrelated to the church. Most who came were friends and family who didn't attend the church. The church had its own home fellowship program set up, and encouraged everyone to get involved. Eventually we felt we should show more commitment to the church and joined the cell group in our neighborhood. But going to two meetings a week was taking too much of our time, so we eventually canceled our own home gathering. I felt like I was abandoning those who had been coming but we just couldn't do both. In hindsight, this was probably a mistake. But it was one that God used to deliver us out of the church bondage once and for all.

One night, as we met with our group, a dispute arose between myself and the appointed group leader over an issue of healing. I believed in healing, as they did, although to be honest I had not yet seen that healing was assured me as part of the salvation package. That *"by his wounds you (we) were healed"* (1 Pet. 2:24). That revelation came later. The issue at this meeting, however, was about a woman in our group with crippling arthritis who had been prayed for but who remained unhealed. It was being suggested, that since the group had done their part by praying and believing, the reason she was still not healed must be her lack of faith. I didn't think that was very loving, and I said so.

A few days later I was invited to a casual lunch at one of the assistant pastor's homes. During the lunch the healing controversy was brought up. (Showing me that the cell groups were just the eyes and ears of the church leaders.) It was suggested I might like to attend one of the teaching seminars on healing that took place just prior to the regular Sunday service. I told him that wouldn't really be convenient for us with four kids and asked why didn't they teach it at the regular service if it was that vital? I forget his answer. I just remember leaving with the feeling that we were not all on the same happy page about whether we were entitled to diasagree or not.

As we heard about other couples in the church being pressured to conform to certain church doctrines or behavioral standards, we became more and more uncomfortable. Finally, on one hot summer Sunday morning as we were sweating through a not particularly meaningful sermon, Mo and I looked at each other, and both our eyes asked, "What are we doing here?" So, gathering up our children, we slipped out a side door. Later we met with the senior pastor and his wife and told them we were going to "pull back" for awhile. We said we'd come occassionally, but not all the time. They weren't thrilled by our decision, but nevertheless agreed to this arrangement and said they'd "cover for us" if anyone asked why we weren't around. I'm not sure why we needed "covering," but that's what they said.

We dropped out for a couple of weeks and then one weekend an old college friend came to visit. In catching him up on our life I mentioned the church and for some reason he said he'd like to see it. So that Sunday I drove him to the service, while Mo chose to stay home with the kids.

Later in the day, after my friend left, a car pulled into the driveway and the senior pastor and one of his junior pastors got out. Surprised to see them, I greeted them and asked what the reason was for their surprise visit? They said they wanted to talk with us about something. I didn't have a good feeling about this, so I decided not to invite them into the house but took them up to the pool area. I called to Mo to come join us and she did.

Taking their seats they quickly got to the point. Basically they wanted a better explanation for why we weren't attending church more regularly. When I explained again that we just felt the need to pull back for awhile, the younger man accused me of spiritual pride. The senior pastor quickly agreed. They both then said that considering our present attitude we would no longer be welcome at the church. And if we did show up, we would not be allowed to use the microphone to say anything.

I felt like I was facing Father Sal all over again. Only this time we were getting the left foot of fellowship Mennonite style—we were being shunned. But even as they passed judgment on us, I knew they couldn't touch us. In our spirits we were free of all their control and condemnation. I also knew this would be the last time we'd have to go through something like this again.

When they had finished delivering their sentence, we walked them to their car, told them we loved them, and gave them a hug in Christian love. As they drove off we waved good-bye to them—and the entire institutional church forever.

It was the summer of 1980, and except for an occassional wedding, funeral or special event we have not graced a pew since. And anytime either Mo or I wonder wistfully out loud if maybe we shouldn't think of joining a church again, there's a momentary pause as we reflect back on all we'd been through, and we just shake our heads, laugh, and say— "No way!"

The Pat Boone miracle "dream" home.

Chapter 13

Reflections

By leaving that church, we had finally accepted what the Lord was trying to show us from the start. That institutional Christianity, with all its steepled, earthly temples, self-appointed hierarchy, unauthorized holy days, traditions and divisions, has absolutely nothing to do with what Jesus came to establish. As we now know, man is the head of this entire church system, not Jesus.

This truth was graphically demonstrated to me years later by the Lord when visiting the Museum of Natural History in New York with my family.

As we entered the dinosaur exhibit, we came upon a tour group standing in front of a towering skeleton of some reptilian creature whose ten-syllable name I have long forgotten. The guide was explaining that the skull on the creature was actually not the real head. Turning to a glass cabinet behind us, she pointed to another skull and said that was the real head. The mistake had been realized years before, but the curator felt the skeleton was too fragile to attempt putting the right head back on the dinosaur.

In a flash, I understood the Holy Spirit was telling me this was the same situation in the institutional church. It has man as its head—not Jesus Christ. And because this structure is so unstable, any attempt to reintroduce the true head of the church to this body would cause the whole thing to collapse. This is what happens during a revival, when the Holy Spirit reclaims His leadership role and our neat, well-programmed religious services collapse in chaos. Which is why He is resisted so much by those who want to keep things decently and in order. Better to preserve the dry bones in their present theological configuration, the thinking goes, than risk a total collapse.

Looking back, I'm amazed how long it took for us to see this. From the moment Jesus told us, "I'm not in there," we had the truth. He then confirmed it over and over to us through the Scriptures, by subsequent revelations of the Spirit, and our own experiences inside the system. Yet we still clung to the romantic notion that the organized church was somehow important to our life with Christ. And refused to see how fraudulent it really was.

It is interesting to me, that except for the Roman Catholic Church, the Lord never specifically told us to leave any of the other church expressions. He had revealed to us up front that He was outside the system, but made no further demands on us. He just let us stay in there until we discovered the lie for ourselves. I believe He did that for only one reason. Because this is all about love. The lover of our souls, Jesus, wants us to choose Him freely. If we choose to stay with another lover, it is our choice. He will not interfere. But He will continue to woo us until we choose to reject the false lover and "*go out to Him outside the camp*" (Heb. 13:13).

The church system comes to us in His name and wants us to think it represents Him. It tells us if we obey it, we show love towards Him. But that is a lie. He never appointed it. It does not represent Him. He is not in there. He never was.

How could it represent Him?

1) It usurps the place of the Holy Spirit with its emphasis on the hierarchy of human leadership.

(2) It divides the body of Christ into an elite clergy that act as our intermediary with God, and a lower-class laity from whom is expected little more than (as author Robert Girard expressed it) "tithe, 'tendence and testimony."

(3) It further divides the body into hundreds of independent denominations grouped around various theologies, charismatic leaders and rituals.

(4) It stifles true Holy Spirit fellowship and ministry among believers with its single speaker/ spectator format.

(5) It keeps individual believers from reaching spiritual maturity by urging us to lean on the provisions of the institution instead of God alone.

(6) It puts guilt and condemnation on the followers of Christ by burdening us with man-made laws and regulations.

(7) It nullifies the word of God with unbiblical traditions.

(8) It reinforces the false idea that a church building is the temple of God.

(9) It robs us of our Hebraic heritage and the inheritance promised to us as the seed of Abraham.

(10) And worst of all, it promotes a religion of works-righteousness that continually undermines our faith and trust in the finished work of Messiah upon which our whole salvation rests.

In short, the organized church represents another gospel, another plan of salvation—another Messiah. In receiving this gospel, a subtle but critical transfer of authority ensues. Instead of relying upon the indwelling voice of the Holy Spirit, the fellowship of believers, and the Word of God to keep us on the straight and narrow, we switch our dependence and loyalty onto someone else's voice. We have empowered the professionals who run the local church complexes to be the guardians of our eternal destiny. And then, having agreed to be part of this salvation plan, we try and build our spiritual house upon a foundation of men's traditions. A foundation that God's Word declares will not be able to withstand the spiritual storms of life, much less bring us into our promised inheritance.

Why didn't Mo and I take Jesus at His word when He first told us the truth? Unbelief—and disbelief. It's one thing to see the lie in an individual church—or in a whole denomination as we did with Roman Catholicism—but it is another to ascribe falseness to the entire Christian church system. It was like being told that a longtime friend of the family is actually a fraud and a cheat. At first you deny it, believing that surely there is a good explanation. Then as the evidence mounts, you become more and more suspect, going back and forth between agreeing with the evidence and shying away from the conclusion it undeniably points to.

A good illustration is the way we dealt with Christmas. After we met the Lord, we became bothered by all the unscriptural traditions surrounding this Christian holiday. In an attempt, therefore, to do it right and restore the focus to Jesus, we tried to turn Christmas into a big "Happy Birthday, Jesus" party. But that soon felt silly.

You see we thought Christmas was a legitimate Christian celebration of the birth of Jesus that had just become somewhat paganized and secularized over the centuries. (Jesus was probably born around the Feast of Tabernacles, in October.) What we finally learned was that December twenty-fifth was actually a pagan holy day of sun worship commemorating the birth of Zeus/Jupiter that had been Christianized over the centuries! Eventually we saw the same thing was true for the entire institutional church system. It too was nothing more than an amalgamation of the world's religious ideas beneath a Christian veneer.

What added to the obfuscation is that the institutional church in all its Catholic and Protestant forms is a master at adapting itself to changing times. It's always working hard to brighten its image and make its programs contemporary and attractive. Just when you think you see it for what it is, it changes chameleon-like into something new and seemingly more relevant and reverent. And then you're not so sure anymore. So you give it another chance.

Another reason we were fooled is because we were always looking at the wrong thing. It's like the joke about the man who would ride his bike to the border each week seeking to cross into the neighboring country. Although the border guard was convinced the man was a smuggler, he could never find any contraband on the man or in the bike's basket. So he would always have to let him pass. Years later, after the guard retired, he spotted the man on the street one day and asked him point blank what he had been smuggling. No longer concerned about being arrested, the man gladly obliged. "Bicycles," he said with a smile.

As long as we keep thinking that the problem is the pastor, or the theology, or the liturgy, or the size of the building, or the style of music, or the types of programs offered, we will be distracted into trying to fix that. And we'll look right past the real problem—the religious system itself. As the oft quoted Marshall McLuhan has said, "The medium is the message." It's the vehicle carrying the message that often speaks louder than the message itself.

Look at the disastrous story of King David trying to return the Ark of the Covenant to Jerusalem using a Philistine ox cart. (See 1 Chronicles 13.) The cart may have been a logical and practical solution to the problem—but it was not the way the Word of God had instructed the Ark to be moved. The Ark was supposed to be carried upon acacia poles, and only by the Levite priests (1 Chron. 15: 2, 13; Ex. 25). The ox cart idea was the way the pagan Philistines had chosen to return the Ark to Israel, and David had also employed it. Sure it will carry you along for awhile, but sooner or later you'll hit a bump in the road and people will begin to die. Our church system is a Philistine ox cart. And I have no doubt that just as God finally stopped David's praise-filled procession dead in its tracks, He will bring this church system to a halt, also. It's just amazing to me that He's let it continue as long as He has.

But probably the biggest obstacle for us was trying to explain all the good the church system does if it's so bad. It preaches the gospel. It sends out missionaries. It instructs on the Bible. It inspires with wonderful worship music. It counsels families. It teaches our children. It supports charities. Plus, our most gifted, spiritual leaders are ministering in there and encourage us to join them. Over and over, we tortured ourselves with the very words that were flung at Martin Luther: "Is the whole church wrong and only we have eyes to see?"

We finally concluded that in spite of the many good things that this religious system does, and the often friendly, spiritual environment it provides, it is a Trojan horse in our midst. In the long run, it does not advance the cause of Christ, it undermines it. It has its own agenda, and almost always takes more than it gives. Including from those who perform its ministry. As Howard Snyder lamented in his ground-breaking analysis of church structure, "It is hard to escape the conclusion that today one of the greatest roadblocks to the gospel of Jesus Christ is the institutional church", (Howard A. Snyder, The Problem of Wineskins, p. 21).

And, oh yes, I don't want to forget Hebrews 10:25. That Scripture was a constant stumbling stone for us. It says: *"Let us not give up meeting together, as some are in the habit of doing, but let us encourage <u>one another</u> – and all the more as you see the Day approaching."*

As <u>interpreted in most churches, this is the ultimate admonition to join a locally organized church and faithfully attend services every Sun</u>day. But notice that nowhere does it tell us where to meet. Or how to meet. Or when to meet. Just that we should meet and keep on meeting. <u>Meet for what? As the rest of the New Testament instructs, to conn</u>ect, <u>to love, to exhort, to bless, to pray for, to encourage and</u> in <u>general to build up one another</u>. This is a much higher level of commitment to fellowship than is experienced in the institutional model, where we only meet once a week for about an hour, sing a few songs, and listen to one man's spiritual point of view, but experience little or no interaction with the other members of Christ's body. Most of whom we don't even know.

And isn't it odd that this admonition is found only in the Book of Hebrews? And not in any of the teaching epistles of Paul regarding "church" life? I believe there's a reason for that—which I just recently discovered. I believe the "gathering" or "meeting together" this verse is really speaking of transcends even meeting for regular fellowship.

The Greek word translated "meeting together" is *"episunagoge,"* which suggests "a complete collection" (Strongs Concordance, #1997). It is a combination of two words: *epi*, a preposition suggesting over, above—at a higher level, as we see in our word "epicenter" or "epic." And *sunago*, from which we get the word "synagogue." Together it suggests the assembling together of all believers in God's super synagogue, or tabernacle. Which is what the writer of

Hebrews is encouraging us to do individually or corporately (as we are able) when he speaks about going through the veil and coming boldly before God's throne. But I believe there is even more here.

This word, a noun, only appears twice in the entire New Testament. The other place is 2 Thessalonians 2:1: *"Concerning the coming of our Lord Jesus Christ and our being gathered to him...."* I'm no Greek scholar, but when I find that a word is only used twice in the Bible, and the other use concerns our being gathered together to Him for the final glorious transfiguration of the saints, that tells me something. It tells me it's not something we do, but something that will be done to us.

Going back to Hebrews, I believe the ultimate "meeting" or "gathering together" spoken about in 10:25 is better understood by going back to verse 23. *"Let us hold unswervingly to the hope we profess, for he who promised is faithful."* If I may translate v. 25 then in context of the whole chapter, it would read like this: *"Let us not give up* (our hope) *of being gathered together* (in Jesus with all our fellow believers, alive or dead), *as some are in the habit of doing, but let us encourage one another– and all the more as you see the Day approaching* (when we will all be made complete in Him in the temple of His body)."

Whether I have this completely correct or not, my point is that this verse in no way justifies an argument for becoming a regular member of an organized church.

Once Mo and I sorted it all out and stopped doubting, we realized that the term that best described our involvement in the institutional church was 'voluntary slavery.' Nobody was forcing us to be in there. Certainly not Jesus. So why stay? When push came to shove we left.

Is there an alternative to the institutional church? Yes, but it's not found in replacing that religious system with a better one. To paraphrase Paul's argument to the Galatians, all religious systems are forms of law which give no life, impart no righteousness and cannot perfect us. If life or righteousness or perfection could be acquired through practicing a system of religious works, Jewish or Christian, then Jesus died for nothing. Because it certainly would have been achieved through practicing the only valid religion that God specifically designed and gave to His people—the Mosaic Law. But as we read in the Book of Hebrews, *"the former regulation is set aside because it was weak and useless, (for the law made nothing perfect), and a better hope is introduced, by which we draw near to God"* (Heb 7:18).

We finally realized we were perfectly capable of drawing near to God in the spirit ourselves without the assistance of the institutional church. It was just as Jesus had declared to the woman at the well after telling her that soon no one would worship God in a particular place, whether at a mountain shrine or in the true temple in Jerusalem. *"Yet a time is coming and has now come when the true worshippers will worship the Father in spirit and truth, for they are the kind of worshippers the Father seeks. God is spirit, and his worshippers must worship in spirit and truth"* (John 4:23,24).

We found we can have a richer, more satisfying spiritual life to the glory of God outside the confines of organized religion than inside. In addition, we avoid all the emotional and spiritual turmoil that comes with trying to reconcile what we believe God is leading us to do and with what certain church leaders think we should or should not be doing. Not that we won't submit to true spiritual authority when we discern it. Or that we don't have true fellowship with other believers. Not at all. We may have departed from Christianity, but not from the Body of Christ.

We understand now that "Christianity" is *"Christ in you, the hope of glory"* (Col 1:27). Nothing less. Nothing more. It is not about trying to do anything for Jesus to secure our salvation, but simply accepting that we are already forgiven and righteous and holy in Him, and obediently letting Him live His life through us by the power of the Holy Spirit. It's a supernatural life, and no one can live it but Him. Any attempt to try and live it in our own religious strength is doomed to failure.

Remember my experience in Kilroy's bar when I was convicted of wearing my religion like a raincoat on Sunday that I took off on Monday? Well that raincoat was nothing more than the tired, old, moth-eaten coat of self-righteousness. It was like the pathetic coat of leaves with which Adam and Eve hastily wrapped themselves. We must begin to see, as Adam hopefully did, that we can never cover the guilt and shame of our sin with the leaves of religious self effort. And to stop trying. Only the Lord can provide for us a proper covering. For Adam He provided an animal skin, paid for with the blood of the animal. For as the Scriptures say, *"Without the shedding of blood, there is no forgiveness"* (Heb. 9:22). But for us, the new Adam, He has provided a beautiful, though presently invisible, *"robe of righteousness"* (Isaiah 61:10 NAS). Paid for this time with His own precious blood.

We must simply gird our loins with the truth and by faith "put on" this priceless nature of righteousness that cost Him so much. At the same time we must have the courage to lay aside the religious rags we've been wearing. We may have to walk naked before the world and endure the slurs of religious folks, but in His sight and ours, we will never be dressed more regally.

Over the years Mo would always say to me, "it's just Jesus." And I would say, "yes, but what about this? Or what about that? We can't ignore all those important biblical truths, can we?" But you know, Mo was right. It's not even about doing the right thing, or believing the right thing, as important as those things are. It all really comes down to having an intimate, loving relationship with Jesus! If we concentrate on that, to quote a line from a Keith Green song, *"He'll take care of the rest."*

Today, we worship and pray and serve Jesus whenever and wherever—and with whomever He puts in our path. Sometimes we meet on the phone. Sometimes in the supermarket. Sometimes in a small home gathering. Sometimes at a large Christian conference. Because as Jesus told us, *"where two or three come together in My name, there am I with them"* (Matt. 18:20). And we remember that the worship Jesus wants most is not found in our songs and words of praise, but in giving up control of our lives to follow Him in obedience each day. As Paul encourages us: *"I urge you therefore, brethren, by the mercies of God, to present your bodies a living and holy sacrifice, acceptable to God, which is your spiritual service of worship"* (Rom. 12:1 NAS).

So that is what we are doing and will continue to do until He comes again to set up His kingdom! I don't think we'll have long to wait.

Chapter 14

A New Beginning

Since I'm sure many will wonder how God finally transitioned us back into the world, I will conclude our tale. This part of our story is actually the most painful to write. As I indicated earlier, I eventually disobeyed the Lord and it cost me—and my family—dearly. My underlying impatience to see God's calling on my life realized caused me to stop doing the work He had given me to do. It happened like this.

If you recall, the Lord indicated in the vision of the Empire State Building that I was to do whatever came to hand and do it with excellence and enthusiasm. That I was not to go looking for work. That He would give me plenty to do. True to His word, an opportunity soon opened up for us to become distributors for Successful Living, a Christian company that provided inspirational books and music.

These products we sold at home gatherings, similar to the way a Tupperware party worked. A person would invite a number of their friends to their house, usually in the evening, and then we'd present the latest Christian books and records on the market and take their orders. It was both a business and a ministry, and we found it very rewarding. Plus it helped us get to know a good cross-section of the Christian community in our area, because everyone who hosted a party for us would usually invite folks from their church circle.

The Lord even did a neat miracle to jump start us in the business. Driving down the road one day, we noticed a garage sale taking place in a fairly well-to-do neighborhood.

Curious, we parked and walked back to the house to see what they were selling. When the owner welcomed us, I noticed he was about my size, and that he had several three-piece suits hanging on a rack. When I looked closer I could see they were all expensive, fashionable, well-tailored suits. The man said I could have the suits for ten dollars apiece. Although $30 was a lot for us to spend, I disparately needed some new clothes, especially if I was going to be a salesman for Successful Living. And how could you beat that price?

When I finally tried the suits on at home they fit perfectly, not requiring even the slightest alteration. That was amazing, because I have a small frame and always have trouble finding clothes that fit. But not when God is my tailor!

For the next year and a half, Mo and I threw ourselves into selling Christian books. Even our two oldest children, Tara and Chris, loved helping us by sorting and packing the orders when they came in. Over the months our business grew, earning us a small, but steady income. But because it was never enough to pay all our bills, the Lord would supplement our income with either faith gifts from friends or by other means.

Once, when Mo was in the supermarket and realized she didn't have enough money to buy what she needed, a total stranger came up to her and said the Lord had just told him to give her this, and handed her forty dollars. Another time a ten dollar bill fluttered past her windshield driving down the street, so she stopped and went back and picked it up. Thank you Jesus! For a while Mo even cleaned house for an elderly gentlemen.

In retrospect, we saw that the Lord was slowly transitioning us from a total faith walk back into the everyday world of earned income. But at the time I didn't see it that way. And the reason I didn't see it was because I didn't want to. Hidden inside me lay an unbroken, willful resistance to going in that direction, because I saw it as carrying me further away from my "calling."

Soon the Lord sent along another employment opportunity for me. It started when a neighbor, who owned a pest control business, complained to me one day how he had to let a man go for dishonesty and was now in a bind. I assured him God would meet his need and even prayed for him while we were standing there. Little did I realize I would be the answer to my own prayer. Because the next day he came back and offered me the job. It would just be part time and I'd have to wear a uniform. The pay would be four dollars an hour. Was I interested?

Realizing the Lord was providing us with another source of income, I told him, "sure, why not?" So now I was doing pest control three days a week, and book parties whenever Mo and I could schedule them. I'd tell anybody who asked, "I do books and bugs and Bible studies on the side."

Life was good at the mansion, as we called the farmhouse. The kids loved living there with the barn and the pasture and all the animals, and even though we were just scraping by financially, Mo and I were content. It was a wonderful godly area, thanks to its Mennonite influence, with good schools and a caring, hard-working community. We couldn't have picked a better place to raise a family. And we were full of praise to God for sending us here.

However, as our second Christmas in the house drew near, and our financial situation remained static, I began to lose my focus. That unbroken will that was hidden within me began rising to the surface. I started to chafe at the low return I was getting on my labor and the constant struggle to make ends meet. I was also becoming frustrated again by the slow development of "my ministry," forgetting the Lord's instructions to leave that to Him and just concentrate on what came to hand. Before long I had convinced myself (and Mo) that this hand-to-mouth phase of our life was coming to a close and the Lord was about to open His promised door of ministry for us.

In an effort to help God move things along, I told Mo I thought we should "tithe" all our book profits to our customers by selling them for cost. This sacrificial giving, I reasoned, would no doubt result in a greater financial blessing from God. But it didn't. It only made matters worse. In reality, I was trying to maneuver God into a position of where He'd have to reward us or rescue us. But as I discovered the hard way, God will never allow us to put Him in our debt.

In January, my pest-control employer approached me and said he wanted to expand my part-time job to a full-time job, was I interested? Even though it would provide two more days of much-needed income, I was now fully committed to my belief that God was finally phasing us out of this minimum-wage existence into the long-awaited ministry, so I declined his offer. So my career as an exterminator ended that day. Now we were back to zero income again. And it didn't take long before we were falling behind on the rent.

When we were two months in arrears, a polite but probing phone call arrived from the Lupinacci family wondering what was going on. I apologized profusely for being late and assured them we'd pay every penny. I then walked out in the pasture and cried out to God for help. Although I kept waiting for His miraculous provision to appear as before, the heavens remained silent. A few weeks later Richard called and suggested that if I painted the house he'd apply my labor to the rent. So I agreed, and that helped a bit. In time, I painted the whole house which paid for two or three months rent. But we still kept sinking. We knew we were putting pressure on the Lupinaccis to cover our rent to protect their credit rating. But trapped in my mindset as I was, I could do nothing but sit and wait. Every day was an agony.

If things weren't awkward enough, a younger brother of Richard's, Kenny Lupinacci, was planning to be married on the front lawn of the farm that July. Which meant the whole Lupinacci clan would be here for a wedding in a couple of months. Even more embarrassing, Kenny, who had become a believer while attending our weekly Bible study, had asked me to be his best man! I could just imagine the pall my unpaid rent situation was going to cast upon the whole happy occasion. The situation looked bleak. But then, at the eleventh hour, the Lord had mercy on me, and a check arrived in the mail from my father that was large enough to cover all our back rents. That removed all the tension and the whole event became a joyous affair for everyone.

However, with the wedding behind us a feeling of finality settled into my spirit that I couldn't shake. It was as if the wedding had been more of a climatic event than I realized.

A few days later a strange car pulled into the driveway and a middle-aged couple got out who I'd never seen before. They said they had always admired the house from the road and were curious about its history. I told them what I knew, and even showed them around inside. But as they drove away I had a weird feeling in the pit of my stomach. So did Mo, who said quietly, "I wished you hadn't shown them the inside."

Sure enough, about a week after that I got a call from Richard saying he'd been contacted by a man who wanted to buy the house. Richard told me he really didn't want to sell, but if we didn't think we could keep up with the rent he might be forced to. I told him to do whatever he thought best, because as things stood I couldn't guarantee I wouldn't miss another payment.

When I hung up I knew the Lord was setting something into motion that would extricate us from our deteriorating situation. At that point I still didn't fully understand why we were in the mess we were in. I just knew that something had gone dreadfully wrong and that this was both a judgment and an act of mercy from God.

As I feared, the house was sold and the settlement was scheduled for September. We had about seven weeks to find another place to live. I can't even begin to describe the emotions we all experienced as we started packing in preparation to leave "our home." The kids were devastated. As were Mo and I. I had looked on this house as God's replacement for the one we'd left in Connecticut. Plus, it was linked to the miraculous Pat Boone deliverance that had brought us here, which meant every time someone marveled at the house we had a chance to tell them about the saving power of our God. The house was part of our testimony, and I didn't think we'd ever move again. Now we were being forced out. In some small way, I felt like I was touching the pain and anguish the Jewish people must have felt when they were driven from their beloved city of Jerusalem by the Babylonians, and later by the Romans.

Although reeling from the humiliation and confusion of this move, I continued to cling to my faith that the Lord would take care of us. I knew He would never leave us or forsake us. And He didn't. First, Kathy and Jerry took us in for a few weeks, letting us store our stuff in the barn. We kept the kids in the same schools, so we had to drive them back and forth each day from Quakertown to Telford. In the meantime, our friend and mentor in the book ministry, Ed Kabakjian, provided some part time employment for us in his book warehouse. Finally, we learned of a Christian family who had a home to rent not far from where our house had been in Telford. After interviewing us, they agreed to let us move in, even knowing I had no real job or source of income. God was still with us!

As we tried to rebuild our lives once again, Mo began studying for her real estate license, which would blossom into a successful 25-year career (at last count) in that field. I, on the other hand, realized I had nowhere else to go but back into advertising. And this time I knew that was definitely the Lord's will. Thankfully I still had my portfolio and resume, so I began setting up job interviews with ad agencies in and around Philadelphia. In less than two weeks I landed a job with one of the best agencies in the area at the same salary I had been earning when I left New York.

I reentered the advertising world in December of 1982, six and a half years after we'd boarded the Little Champ in Stamford, Connecticut. I was shocked to see how much things had changed in that short time. Carbon paper was out, and the Xerox copier was in. All my TV commercials, which were on film, now had to be converted to video tape so the agencies could view them. Nobody had film projectors anymore. But the biggest change I discovered had taken place in me. I felt like a Robinson Caruso, who having lived outside the harsh realities of the world system for a time, now found himself thrust once again into the scrambling, graceless rush of civilization.

Valley of the Steeples

Although the people at the agency were wonderful, I immediately became uncomfortable with the working procedure which was at odds with my experience in New York. There a copywriter worked directly with the art director in a team effort. Here, the writer was expected to work on his own ideas independently, and then submit it to the art director for his or her artistic embellishments. Having been away so long from the discipline of creating ideas, I found myself with no one to lean on. Fear quickly overtook me, as I struggled to regain my footing in this familiar, yet unfamiliar, world.

The worst part, however, was the daily condemnation I lived under feeling I had failed God. It was a condition the Devil took full advantage of by telling me constantly that I had been discarded by God as unfit for ministry and was now on my own. Feeling rejected, I was stripped of my faith to rely on God for help.

I was soon getting up two or three hours earlier each day to pray and read my Bible to gain the courage just to go to work. It would be months before the grace of God would break through the stronghold of fear that gripped me to comfort me and remind me, *"that God works all things together for good"* (Rom 8:28). And that included even my failures. I realized again that His love for me had never ceased for one minute. And that, yes, He knew my time on the farm would come to this, so it was no surprise to the Almighty. He had already worked it into His plan for my life. His words to me in essence were, *"relax, see this work in advertising as sent from Me, do it with all your might, trust in Him, and this time don't quit."*

Years later the Lord showed me how I had stumbled. I call it the Parable of the Stupid Goat.

Parable of the Stupid Goat

Brian Hennessy

I would occasionally tell friends an amusing story about a goat we kept in the pasture. About how one day I watched this goat stick his head through one of the squares formed by the horizontal and vertical wires in the fence to nibble on our lawn. It was the proverbial case of the grass being greener in the other fellow's yard. But then, when he tried to pull his head back through the fence, I saw he couldn't. His curved horns hooked on the fence to block his retreat.

Seeing he needed help, I climbed into the pasture to free him. After trying a few things that didn't work, I realized if I tilted his head back to flatten the horns, then turned it sideways, I could slide him back through the opening. As he scampered off I told him not to be so stupid next time and clambered back out of the pasture.

But he didn't listen too well. The next day I came out to find him again with his head stuck in the fence, this time clear on the other side of the pasture. Lord only knows how long he'd been there. So once more I climbed into the pasture and went through the same head-twisting motions to free him. This soon became a regular routine with us. When I asked one of the local farmers about it, he said, "Oh, goats are stupid. They never learn." So I gave up hope he'd ever change. My biggest fear was some stray dog would find him in that vulnerable position and kill him.

One day, I had a brilliant idea. I taped a long wooden dowel across his horns with duct tape to prevent him from fitting his head through the fence to begin with. But he was determined, and he soon had the dowel dangling from one horn.

Finally, I'd had enough. I told Stupid Goat, as we now called him, that if he did it one more time, he was going into the classified section of the local newspaper. Maybe he wanted to see his name in the paper, I don't know, but two days later he was stuck in the fence again. "That does it," I yelled. "You are now officially for sale!" But as I stood there fuming, Stupid Goat suddenly tilted his horns back, turned his head sideways and pulled his head back through the fence. I couldn't believe my eyes! He had learned! He wasn't stupid after all! And from then on that's what he would do.

After relating that tale again one day, the Lord spoke to me and said, *"You were that goat."*

In an instant, I understood. Like the goat, I had gotten my head stuck in the fence trying to get to my ministry. I had forgotten the first lesson He'd taught me up in New York about not trying to escape the pasture He puts us in, but to wait for Him to open the gate. But I realized his point in showing this to me was to remind me that the goat had learned! Which meant, so had I! In that moment I could sense the warmth of my Father's proud smile, and I beamed with pleasure. *"It is for discipline that you endure; God deals with you as with sons, for what son is there whom his father does not discipline?...all discipline for the moment seems not to be joyful, but sorrowful; yet to those who have been trained by it, afterwards it yields the peaceful fruit of righteousness"* (Heb. 12:7-11 NAS).

Even though that first year back in advertising was probably the most difficult year of my life, with God's help I persevered and our life began to stabilize. Soon, we were able to buy a new, four-bedroom twin close to where we'd been living. And five years later we could afford to built a home on an acre of wooded ground in the area.

Although I eventually lost that first job in advertising about a year later because of my early shakiness, that simply allowed God to move me to another agency in downtown

Philadelphia for more money, and which was better suited to my style of working. I quickly settled into this more compatible working environment and remained with that company for another twenty years.

Throughout those years, I never forgot God's great calling on my life, but like the goat, I learned how to stick my head into ministry occasionally without getting stuck. As Paul boasted late in life, *"I have learned to be content whatever the circumstances"* (Phil 4:11).

In 2004, the Lord opened the door for me to leave advertising again, I think for the last time, transitioning me to real estate to join my wife in ReMax as "The Hennessy Team." The Team has since been expanded to include our oldest son, Chris, whose contagious enthusiasm keeps us energized.

As for our other three children, Tara manages a large, local dental practice today, supervising a staff of over fifty technicians and administrators, plus five busy dentists. Brendan is a skilled craftsman and main foreman for a commercial builder in the area. And Todd has become a successful mortgage loan officer, who we see at many of our closings. They are all married, except Todd, who is engaged and plans to be married in September of '08. And to date they have given us seven beautiful grandchildren: Kyle, Jared, Jonah, Sarah, Aidan, Kiera and Connor.

All our children will testify this entire saga, as best they can recall, is the gospel truth.

The Family, 2007

A Word to the Wise

Now that you have heard our story, and all our reasons for leaving the organized church, I want to conclude with this final word.

As I explained throughout this book, the underlying premise for us stepping off the church bus was the discovery that Christianity is a religion that sprang from the false teaching of gentile leaders who wrote in the early centuries. Their teachings, which were too often based upon pagan or worldly concepts, eventually corrupted the way the church was to gather together, relate to one another and minister. Eventually it corrupted even the salvation message itself, turning what was a simple gospel of reconciliation between God and man through faith in Jesus, into a burdensome, idolatrous, religious system. It is seen most clearly in the establishment of the Roman Catholic Church.

I don't claim any exclusivity to seeing this development. Although it was a Holy Spirit revelation to me, God has always had His witnesses to this truth in every age. Sir Robert Anderson, a former chief of Scotland Yard and a great nineteenth-century Christian teacher, wrote, "No fair-minded man would deny that, with very few exceptions, the errors of the Romish system are the fruit of the evil seed of Patristic teaching. Nor can it be denied that many of these evil doctrines appear in the formularies of the National Church (of England)" (Types in Hebrews, p. 155).

As I further stated, and to which Anderson alludes, the Reformation did not completely deliver us from the fruit of "this evil seed." Although the Reformers restored the gospel and jettisoned many doctrinal errors, they left the church system virtually in tact. It just became decentralized into many different national, regional and cultural expressions. From an organizational standpoint, it truly was just a reformation of the same old thing. Mother had simply spawned many daughters.

Tragically, the Reformers didn't seem to realize how important church organization is to the gospel of Jesus Christ. Although the message of salvation through faith in Jesus is the heart of the Gospel (called soteriology by the theologians), it is not the whole gospel. For just as a human heart cannot exist without a human body, so too, a spiritual heart redeemed by the message of salvation needs the true spiritual body of Messiah in which to function. That's why a correct understanding of the form of the church (called ecclesiology) is so vital because it reveals how each believer is to function within Christ's *spiritual* body.

And sure enough, it wasn't long after the Reformation that the leaven began its insidious work again. The reformed churches began to act with the same religious intolerance towards others as Rome had towards them. Their merciless persecution of the Anabaptists, who simply wanted to be rebaptized as believing adults, added to the shed blood for which this false church will one day be held accountable. The only reason mayhem in the name of Christ has been kept to a minimum these last few centuries is because the power of the state was finally blocked from enforcing church doctrine in Western civilization. Emotional and sexual abuse may abound today, but as bad as that is, at least nobody has been burned at the stake in awhile. (Ironically, the state is being united to a national religion today in that it is enforcing the religious beliefs of secular humanism in this and many other countries.)

Nevertheless, just because things have been quiet doesn't mean the corrupting influence of the leaven hasn't been steadily at work within the so-called Protestant churches. Polls are constantly showing that the evangelical church is proportionately no different from the unbelieving world when it comes to participating in abortions, divorces, homosexuality, pornography, and scorn for absolute Biblical values, revealing the hidden, growing presence of the death principle.

Nobody defines it with more sobering clarity than A. W. Tozer, writing in the mid-1950s: "Because of long and meticulous organization it is now possible for the youngest pastor just out of seminary to have more actual authority in a church than Jesus Christ has....Among the gospel churches Christ is now in fact little more than a beloved symbol." And as a pastor, he acknowledged "that I am myself very much involved in the situation I here deplore" (The Best of A.W. Tozer, pgs 87- 89).

Here then is my word to the wise.

The leavening process is almost complete and will soon cause the whole institutional loaf of bread to rise up again with its characteristic murderous intolerance for the truth. Jesus warned us this would happen in His kingdom parables, as recorded in the thirteenth chapter of Matthew's gospel.

It's important to understand that when Jesus refers to the kingdom of heaven in these parables He is speaking about us. As He told us, *"the kingdom of God is within you"* (Luke 17:21). So when He talks about this kingdom of heaven becoming corrupted, He means the kingdom as represented externally by the church on earth.

One parable states: *"The kingdom of heaven may be compared to a man who sowed good seed in his field. While men were sleeping, his enemy came and sowed tares among the wheat, and went away"* (Matt. 13:24,25 NAS). I believe this refers to when the original Jewish apostles and prophets died – or "slept," and the church was soon contaminated by the lie of the enemy that came in primarily through the church fathers. And because that lie has not been sufficiently confronted and eradicated, it will blossom once again until we all finally see it for what it is and repent. That's what Jesus meant when He said *"The kingdom of heaven is like leaven, which a woman took and hid in three pecks of meal, until it was all leavened"* (Matt. 13:33 NAS).

So, I believe, this is where we are headed. There are two bodies of Christians in the world today, both claiming to be Christ's body. One is an organism and the other is an organization. One group is clinging to Jesus as the living head of the church, and the other is clinging to a lifeless, man-made system. One group is alive, and the other is dead. And most of the time it's hard to know who is who. Because although there are many believers like my family who are outside the system, most of the true followers of Christ are still inside sharing a pew with those who are not on the same team. *"For if anyone does not have the Spirit of Christ, he does not belong to Him"* (Rom. 8:9 NAS).

This mixture of believers and unbelievers in the institutional church is the result of trying to provide for both saint and sinner through what is called "public worship." But a house divided against itself cannot stand. *"For what fellowship can light have with darkness?...What does a believer have in common with an unbeliever?"* (2 Cor. 6:14,15). So a shaking is coming that will soon separate us into our rightful bodies. But the shaking will not result in Jesus becoming the head of the institutional church. I know many true believers think this will happen, because that is what they are praying and fasting for when they cry out for revival to take hold in their dead and dying congregations. But God will never glorify that which He did not ordain.

But hasn't He done so in the past, you might ask, when He brought great revivals? No. All the great revivals He brought were to awaken us to the truth about this religion so we would discard it. The word "revival" itself implies we are near death and need to be revived. But whenever revival came, instead of seeing that it was our religion that had brought the death, we went right back and started it up all over again with a new, improved theology.

I believe the words of Paul to the Athenians, who loved to worship in temples made by human hands, apply to us today. *"In the past God overlooked such ignorance, but now he commands all people everywhere to repent. For he has set a day when he will judge the world with justice by the man he has appointed. He has given proof of this to all men by raising him from the dead"* (Acts 17:30).

What lies ahead? We have two sets of dry bones trying to come to life. Although the true body of Christ may be alive with the spirit of God, it is just barely so. As a walking, talking, miracle-working, holy powerhouse of resurrection life on this earth, we are as disconnected and useless as the dry bones Ezekiel saw lying scattered about on the valley floor. But that is soon going to change. As the prophecy states, *"Behold, I will cause breath to enter you that you may come to life"* (Ezek 37:5 NAS).

And look what happens when the breath of the Holy Spirit does come upon us: *"So I prophesied as he commanded me, and the breath came into them, and they came to life, and stood on their feet, an exceedingly great army. Then He said to me, 'Son of man, these bones are the whole house of Israel'"* (Ezek 37: 10, 11 NAS). I have no doubt this is the army the Lord showed me on the night He first revealed Himself to me (see page 24).

It is also the *"one new man"* that Paul spoke about in Ephesians 2:15; the fullness of the gentiles who have been grafted into Israel combined with the soon-to-be awakened Jewish remnant. That is what Jesus prayed for when He asked the Father *"that they may be one as we are one"* (John 17:21). Ephraim and Judah united again. Together we will become God's force for righteousness on earth as the restored Israel of God. This is the *"manifestation of the sons of God"* (Rom. 8:19 NAS) who have attained *"to the unity of the faith, and of the knowledge of the Son of God, to a mature man to the measure of the stature, which belongs to the fullness of Christ"* (Eph. 4:13). It is the resurrected life of Jesus manifested in us coming forth as the Son of David, Israel's Messiah and Commander and Chief.

Clearly we are headed for new revitalization!

But so is the camp of the enemy. The dead bones of that institutional dinosaur are going to come to life again, as well.

Ask yourself, if we belong to the true body of Jesus, whose body can that other group be a part of? Especially when you recall that the institutional church specifically claims to be the true body of Christ, which it is not. Who else but the false christ, the false messiah—the one called Antichrist? Is it any wonder that the command given in Revelation is so urgent? *"Come out of her, my people, that you may not participate in her sins and that you may not receive of her plagues"* (Rev. 18:4 NAS).

Soon, I believe, we will see the institutional church become worse than it was during the Dark Ages. Satan will come to his body like the demon in the parable Jesus told, who having been cast out of his house, returns to find it swept clean, *"and brings along seven other spirits more wicked than itself. And the last state... becomes worse than the first"* (Matt. 12: 43-45 NAS).

Somehow Satan will unify the denominations, both Catholic and Protestant, probably in combination with all the other cults and religions. It will then go forth with great miracle-working power to deceive the world. We can see signs of this happening already in many parts of the so-called Emerging Church (or e-merging church) with its openness to eastern mysticism and political correctness. On the surface, this all-embracive entity will appear to be the true body of Christ, but it will be anything but that. It will be mixture—which translated means "Babylon."

In her, Dame Babylon will finally be revealed in all her seductive splendor. *"And the woman was clothed in purple and scarlet, and adorned with gold and precious stones and pearls, having in her hand a gold cup full of abominations and of the unclean things of her immorality, and upon her forehead a name was written, a mystery, 'BABYLON THE GREAT, THE MOTHER OF HARLOTS AND OF THE ABOMINATIONS OF THE EARTH"* (Rev. 17:4,5 NAS).

It seems she will ally herself with the political powers, uniting church and state again, but her glory will be short lived. Her long overdue punishment is at hand. *"In one day her plagues will overtake her; death mourning and famine, She will be consumed by fire, for mighty is the Lord God who judges her"* (Rev. 18:8).

The temptation is to think, "Oh, my church wouldn't be a part of that. We have a very loving, Christ-centered fellowship." You may well have, but it doesn't change anything. If you are part of the system, you are in the wrong camp.

Valley of the Steeples

The other temptation is to think that Christianity cannot possibly be Mystery Babylon because it is a relatively new religion. Don't kid yourself. Christianity is in fact the very same "old-time religion" that has plagued mankind since the Fall. It is simply operating in its latest disguise. A big clue to the ancient identity of this religion is in the vision the Lord gave to my wife that inspired the title of this book.

If you recall, the one thing that symbolically unified all the churches in the valley was the "steeple." Did you ever wonder why churches have steeples? Historically, it could be argued, they were constructed to house a bell that called the people to service. But why continue to incorporate architecture for such an outdated function today? True, steeples are very picturesque, especially as you drive around New England. And if you're looking for a church, they make it easy to quickly locate one in town.

Nostalgia and tradition aside, however, the hidden reason churches have steeples is because they hearken back to the mother of all churches—the Tower of Babel. That first church, which so arrogantly aspired to reach the heavens, was so displeasing to God that He dramatically halted all construction on it by confusing the languages of the church planning commission. As the people then moved on from Babylon, they took the idolatrous tower idea with them. Ralph Woodrow, in his powerful book, Mystery Babylon, does a marvelous job of tracing how this phallic symbol of sun worship reappears as the ziggurats of later Babylon, as the obelisks of Egypt, as the minarets of Islam, as the pagodas of oriental religions, and as the lofty spires of Christian cathedrals.

Most church members would be horrified to learn that their lovely steeple is a link to the Tower of Babel, even worse, a phallic symbol. Nevertheless, the unbroken continuation of this mysterious tradition speaks for itself. And remember, the real horror is not the steeple, as odious as that devoted thing is in the nostrils of God. To the discerning believer, a steeple reveals the true identity of the religion served within the building upon which it sits—Mystery Babylon.

Can we not see that that our church buildings with their Babylonian steeple towers thrusting themselves upward into the face of God, are the spiritual descendants of the so-called high places? Those places of idolatry, where the people sacrificed and burned incense, were a continual snare to Israel. The nation would not let go of them. Even the few good kings who ruled Israel, except for Hoshea, allowed them to remain. Over and over you read in their biblical obituaries that *"they did right in the sight of the Lord...only the high places were not taken away"* (2 Kings 15:3,4 NAS).

Listen to the prophet Ezekiel take Israel to task for these high places, and see if you don't recognize them in our cities and towns today. *"And after all your wickedness (woe, woe to you! Says the Lord God) you have built also for yourself a vaulted chamber, and made yourself a high place in every square at the head of every street you built your high place and prostituted your beauty..."* (Ezek 16:23-25 RSV).

The bottom line, whether we want to admit it or not, is our church buildings represent "the work of our hands." They are symbolically no different than the golden calf that Israel built to worship the god who brought them out of Egypt. They stand as mute testimony to our carnal, religious mindset. They declare our unbelief in the finished work of Jesus Christ. They reveal we have believed a lie.

But once you see it, you see it. And you realize that the very same religion that caused our forefathers to stumble, has deceived us as well. The words of Jeremiah wail to us across the centuries: *"But the shameful thing has consumed the labor of our fathers since our youth, their flocks and their herds, their sons and their daughters. Let us lie down in our shame, and let our humiliation cover us; for we have sinned against the Lord or God, we and our fathers, since our youth even to this day. And we have not obeyed the voice of the Lord our God"* (Jer. 3:24, 25 NAS).

Hear then, the voice of the Lord today:

"Come out of her, my people, that you may not participate in her sins and that you may not receive of her plagues. For her sins have piled up as high as heaven, and God has remembered her iniquities" (Rev. 18:4, 5 NAS).

Brian Hennessy's web site is:
www.BHennessy.com

He can be contacted at:
Brian@BHennessy.com

Sources and Recommended Reading:

Anderson, Sir Robert. <u>Types in Hebrews</u>. Kregal Publications, 1978

Bainton, Roland H. <u>Here I Stand, A Life of Martin Luther</u>. Abington Press, 1950

Cook, Jerry. <u>Love, Acceptance and Forgiveness</u>. Regal Press, 1979

Gillham, Bill. <u>Lifetime Guarantee</u>. Harvest House Publishers, 1987

Girard, Robert C. <u>Brethren, Hang Loose!</u> Zondervan, 1972

Girard, Robert C. <u>Brethren, Hang Together!</u> Zondervan, 1979

Hislop, Alexander. <u>The Two Babylons</u>. Loizeaux Brothers, 1959

Law, William. <u>The Power of the Spirit</u>. Christian Literature Crusade, 1971

McVey, Steve. <u>Grace Walk</u>. Harvest House Publishers, 1995

McVey, Steve. <u>Grace Rules</u>. Harvest House Publishers, 1998

Nee, Watchman. <u>Sit, Walk, Stand</u>. Tyndale House Publishers, 1977

Rutz, James. <u>Mega Shift</u>. Empowerment Press, 2005

Slosser, Bob. Miracle in Darien. Logos International, 1979

Smith, Hannah Whitehall. The God of All Comfort, Moody Press, 1956

Snyder, Howard A. The Problem of Wine Skins. Inter-Varsity Press, 1976

Wiersbe, Warren W. The Best of Tozer. Baker Book House, 1978

Wolston, W.T.P. The Church: What is it?, Bible Truth Publishers, 1982

Woodrow, Ralph. Babylon Mystery Religion, Ralph Woodrow Evangelistic Association. Inc., 1977